PLANTATION HOMES OF LOUISIANA

Edited by
NANCY HARRIS CALHOUN
JAMES CALHOUN
HELEN KERR KEMPE

PELICAN PUBLISHING COMPANY
GRETNA 1986

CONTENTS

TOUR 1

The Garden District

New Orleans is a city eternally in bloom; almost every variety of plant life thrives in its warm, humid climate and fertile, alluvial soil. Flowering seasons continually overlap, and there is never a day that passes when beautiful flowers are not blooming in some garden.

The New Orleans GARDEN DISTRICT, planned in the early 1820's, resembled a huge park; but much of the original beauty has faded through the years. Many lovely gardens are still to be seen, and should be included in the itinerary of every New Orleans visitor.

THE GARDEN DISTRICT is generally located in the area bounded by Jackson Avenue and Louisiana Avenue — east to west; and St. Charles Avenue and Magazine Street — north to south.

Audubon Park

This beautiful 247-acre park now stands on what once was the Foucher Plantation and the Boré Plantation, the latter distinguished by the fact that its owner first granulated sugar commercially there in 1795. A statue of John James Audubon may be seen, as well as gardens, an amusement center and the zoo.

On St. Charles Avenue, across from Tulane University.

5

Westfeldt House

A square, white raised cottage, this structure was built about 1830 for Thomas Toby and probably is one of the oldest buildings in this part of New Orleans.

A beautiful live oak on the grounds is a frequent subject for artists. Private.

At 2340 Prytania Street.

Sanctuary Plantation

This old West Indies style home that was for many years the Walter Parker residence, was purchased by the Benjamin F. Erlangers in the early 1970s, who have restored the home after many years of neglect. The site was once part of the Bayou St. John properties of Don Almonester y Roxas, who sold it in 1793 to Don Luis Antonio Blanc, who in turn sold it to his son in 1816.

A sketch by Charles Alexander Le Sueur about 1830 indicates that the house may have been a one-story structure with gabled ends.

At 924 Moss Street.

De Matteo House

Although popularly known as the Old Spanish Custom House, there is no evidence that this structure ever was used for such a purpose. The land on which the house stands was purchased in 1771 by Juan Renato Huchet de Kernion. This is a fine example of the West Indies style and is quite similar to another house built by Barthelemy Lafon on Bayou St. John Road in 1806.

The house is owned by Dr. and Mrs. Ignatius de Matteo, who have made extensive renovations and added a primitive kitchen and oven in the rear yard. Private.

At 1300 Moss Street.

Holy Rosary Rectory

Built about 1834, this home was later donated for use as a parish church, parsonage and school. Notable features are the fence, well-detailed entrance doors, columns and dormers and the graceful balustrade of the Captain's Walk that surmounts the overhanging roof.

The side galleries are supported from the roof by iron rods instead of columns, as on the front. The five Ionic columns of the entrance doorways and other details from the 1830s indicate the Greek Revival influence. Records indicate that Evariste Blanc purchased the land from David Olivier in 1835. It is now the rectory of Our Lady of the Holy Rosary. Private.

At 1342 Moss Street.

Wisner House

This beautiful raised cottage of the late Greek Revival period, probably dating from the 1850s, is said to have housed in 1882 the first fencing club in New Orleans. It also is reputed to have been the headquarters of a famous rowing club. Private.

At 1347 Moss Street.

Pitot House

(OPEN TO PUBLIC)
Listed in the National Register of Historic Places, Pitot House has been restored by the New Orleans Chapter of the Louisiana Landmarks Society.

Built around 1799 and purchased in 1810 by James Pitot, the second mayor of New Orleans, the house was moved from its original location in 1964.

Open Thursday only, 11-2; nominal entrance fee.

At 1440 Moss Street.

Wilkinson Home

This fine Greek Revival house once was the property of Evariste Blanc. Blanc had purchased the property from the succession of Etienne Reine in 1847, and the present house was constructed some time after that date.

The Robert Musgrove family owned it from 1859 until 1882. It is now owned by the Wilkinson family. Private.

At 1454 Moss Street.

Merieult House

(OPEN TO PUBLIC)

Erected during the Spanish Colonial era by Jean Francois Merieult, this was one of the most elegant homes of its time. It was one of the few remaining structures in the city after the disastrous fire of 1794. The front of the house was added in 1832. Merieult House was completely restored in recent years by Mr. and Mrs. L. Kemper Williams.

The structure now houses The Historic New Orleans Collection, an outstanding treasure of books, paintings, prints, and other artifacts dealing with New Orleans and Louisiana.

Behind the picturesque patio is the Williams home, restored to its original splendor and filled with priceless furnishings.

Listed in the National Register of Historic Places and a member of the American Association of Museums.

Open Tuesday through Saturday, 10-5; nominal entrance fee.

At 533 Royal Street.

Merieult House (Courtesy of The Historic New Orleans Collection, 533 Royal Street)

Marchand House

One of the landmarks of the Vieux Carré, this old home has been restored by Mr. and Mrs. Donald Didier. Its unusual stairway has attracted widespread attention. Private.

At 830 Royal Street.

Gallier House

(OPEN TO PUBLIC)

Not a plantation home, this structure nevertheless is rich in history and once was the home of one of New Orleans' leading 19th century architects, James Gallier, Jr. The home is operated by the Ella West Freeman Foundation as a non-profit educational and tourist attraction.

The main building has been carefully restored with decor and furnishings of the 1860s, the period of Gallier's residency. An auxiliary building also has been renovated to house exhibits from Gallier's era and profession. A third building, now renovated, houses the museum's offices. Mrs. Ann M. Masson is director.

In the restoration of GALLIER HOUSE to its original condition, the ground surrounding the house was sifted for

Gallier House

9

Gallier House Interior

household artifacts of the period. Miss Nadine Carter Russell is curator.

Open Monday through Saturday, 10-4:30; last tour begins at 3:45; nominal entrance fee.

At 1132 Royal Street.

Hermann-Grima House

(OPEN TO PUBLIC)

One of the finest homes in the Vieux Carré, GRIMA HOUSE was built in 1831 by wealthy merchant Samuel Hermann. A Georgian mansion designed by William Brand, it has retained most of its outbuildings, including a stable, open-hearth kitchen, garconniere and courtyard parterre. Now owned by the Christian Women's Exchange, it recently was restored under the direction of noted restoration architect Samuel Wilson, Jr. The house has been refurnished with period antiques and accessories.

Open Monday through Saturday, 10-3:30; Sunday, 1-4:30; tours every half hour beginning at 10 a.m.; nominal entrance fee.

At 820 St. Louis Street.

Madame John's Legacy

(OPEN TO PUBLIC)

The oldest residence in New Orleans, MADAM JOHN'S was not a plantation home, nor a palatial mansion. Its history, however, is marked with mystery and links to Louisiana literature.

The home derives its name from George Washington Cable's celebrated story "Tite Poulette," which featured Madam John, the quadroon mistress of the owner.

The house was built in 1788 and replaces an earlier structure that was destroyed in the great fire which swept the colonial city in that year. It was contracted to be rebuilt shortly after the fire by its owner Don Manuel de Lanzos, a Spanish officer, and Robert Jones, an American builder, who had come to the city earlier from the United States. Its design was the same that had been used by the French in earlier homes. The basement is said to have been a storage place for contraband and a rendezvous for pirates prior to the Lafitte era.

The house was donated to the Louisiana State Museum in 1947 by Mrs. Stella H. Lemann.

Open Tuesday through Sunday, 10-6. Nominal entrance fee. Children under 12, free.

At 632 Dumaine Street.

Lombard Plantation

This old structure is the last remaining example of a creole manor. It was built in 1826 by Joseph Lombard, Sr. for his son and daughter-in-law. At that time the property included a large area of the Vieux Carre, which was later divided and sold to others. The interesting art nouveau brackets now on the gallery are an addition of the 1890s. Private.

At 3933 Chartres Street.

Aurora

The century-old home has round columns supporting a gallery across the front. The roof is supported by slender colonnettes which rise from the second-floor gallery. Private.

Located on Patterson Drive in the Aurora Gardens section of Algiers, West Bank sector of the City of New Orleans.

Belle Chasse

This is the site of the large white square three-story house once owned by Judah P. Benjamin, who served as Secretary of State and Secretary of War for the Confederacy. Prior to joining the Confederacy, he served as a U.S. Senator from Louisiana, 1853-61.

The house was demolished in recent years. However, the bell was saved and has been erected in a special monument by the Plaquemines Parish Commission Council on the original plantation site.

The monument is located in Belle Chasse on Highway 23 immediately in front of the library.

Woodland Plantation House

The present home is not the original structure, although it is quite old. Bradish Johnson, son of one of the owners of MAGNOLIA, was the owner of this house, also known as JOHNSON PLANTATION. He was said to have worn a tall silk hat, Prince Albert coat and striped pants every day.

An interesting feature is the brick slave quarters near the highway. Private.

Off La. 23, two miles above West Pointe a la Hache.

Magnolia Plantation House

Located off the highway in a grove of orange trees is MAGNOLIA PLANTATION HOUSE, built about 1795 by two sea captains — Bradish and Johnson — who had established the plantation there some 15 years earlier.

The house is two-storied, with walls two-and-a-half feet thick on the lower floor and two feet thick on the upper. Eight slender rectangular pillars support the gabled roof.

All work on the house was performed by slave labor, including the hand-carved woodwork.

In 1873 it was purchased by Henry Clay Warmoth, governor of Louisiana — who later built a railroad from Buras to New Orleans. It is now in ruins. Private.

The stack of the old sugar mill still stands.

Off the River Road (La. 23), one-and-a-half miles below West Pointe a la Hache. Take ferry to Pointe a la Hache for Tour 2, to New Orleans.

TOUR 2

Gordon

Situated in a beautiful grove, this simple, raised house was built in 1838 by James Reed Gordon, ancestor of the present occupants. Private.

On the River Road (La. 39), at Carlyle.

Promised Land

This home has now been modernized, although the original section has hand-hewn beams joined with wooden pegs. It is very probable that the original section dates from the early 18th century. Private.

On the River Road (La. 39), below Dalcour.

Mary

This building has been authentically restored to its original design. It is of the Santo Domingo type of West Indies architecture and dates from the 18th century. Private.

On the River Road (La. 39), at Dalcour.

Stella

This plantation home is more than 100 years old. It is a simple brick-and-cypress raised cottage, with a hand-hewn shingled roof overhanging the front gallery, and supported by six square columns.

This home has been restored and modernized. Private.

On the River Road (La. 39), six miles below Braithwaite.

Braithwaite

Built in 1850 by Thomas Morgan, BRAITHWAITE — or ORANGE GROVE — is of unusual architectural design among plantation homes in Louisiana. It is similar to an English-style manor house, complete with Tudor windows and high-pitch gabled roof.

Its name was changed from ORANGE GROVE to BRAITHWAITE when it was purchased by an English syndicate. Now in ruins. Private.

Facing the River Road (La. 39), at Braithwaite.

Kenilworth

This structure was originally a one-story Spanish block-house built in 1759; the second floor was added to it shortly after 1800. The wide galleries which surround the house are supported by massive brick columns, and the roof by cypress colonnettes.

The land on which the plantation is located was owned by the Bienvenue and the Estopinal families, and was frequented by General Beauregard. Popular legends concerning KENILWORTH claim it has ghosts. Private.

On La. 46, five miles east of Poydras.

Beauregard House Museum

(OPEN TO PUBLIC)

Built in the 1830s, this home was later occupied by Judge Rene Beauregard, son of Confederate General P. G. T. Beauregard. The building is of cement-covered brick and has two stories and an attic. Wide upper and lower galleries extend along the front and rear of the home, supported by eight Doric columns. The house was remodeled in 1856 and again in 1865. Both these remodelings are attributed to James Gallier, Jr.

The building was restored in 1957 and is now the headquarters and visitors' center for Chalmette National Historical Park, featuring a museum exhibit and 15-minute audio-visual program on New Orleans and the War of 1812. Located on the site of the Battle for New Orleans, the house gallery offers an impressive view of the battlefield. A one mile tour route, which includes markers, authentic cannon and reconstructed ramparts, and the Chalmette National Cemetery, is adjacent to the site of this house. Free of charge.

Open 8-5, September through May; 8-6, June through August. Closed Christmas and Mardi Gras. Call (504) 271-2412 for information.

On St. Bernard Highway (La. 46), six miles below New Orleans.

Rene Beauregard House

Versailles Site

Pierre Denis de la Ronde, perhaps the wealthiest planter in Louisiana, built this once-imposing mansion, called by contemporaries "The Palace," in 1805. Although only ruins remain today, it rivalled the most magnificent homes of its time.

De la Ronde was an outstanding colonial figure, serving as a lieutenant in the conquest of West Florida, military

15

commandant of St. Bernard, a member of the Cabildo Council from 1778-1803, senator, member of the state Constitutional Convention, colonel on General Andrew Jackson's staff and major general in the Louisiana Militia.

The house was situated about a mile and a half below the plains of Chalmette, at the end of a magnificent avenue of Centenary oaks planted by de la Ronde on his 21st birthday in 1783. It is said to be the finest double-row oak alley in the world.

De la Ronde chose the name VERSAILLES with care, intending it to be a replica of the palace and gardens of Louis XIV. At the lake end of Paris road he planned a city to be named Paris. Damaged and looted during the War of 1812, it was later sold and in 1876 burned to the ground.

Located between the lanes of La. 39, at junction with La. 47.

Lebeau House

Part of a once magnificent plantation, the LEBEAU HOUSE is now an apartment house, badly in need of repair. It was built in 1850 by F. B. Lebeau, and is a two-story brick structure whose outer walls are covered with wood to keep out moisture. A gallery in the front and one in the rear are each supported by eight square wooden columns. Its railings contain very unusual, ornamented ironwork. The hipped roof is surmounted by an octagonal cupola which gives an unobstructed view of the Mississippi. Private.

Just off La. 39 on Friscoville Avenue and Pontalba Street in Arabi. Best seen from the parking lot behind the Disabled Veterans Building.

TOUR 3

Whitehall - Magnolia School

Built in the 1850's by Francois Pascalise de Labarre, this raised cottage is fronted by a wide, columned gallery and set in a grove of magnolias, cedars and live oaks.

During the War Between the States, Federal troops were encamped here.

The home was sold by the Labarres, and was later converted into a gambling house. Still later, the Jesuits converted the house into a Jesuit retreat.

Since 1931 WHITEHALL has served as a boarding school for handicapped children, and is now called MAGNOLIA SCHOOL.

On U. S. 90 (River Road) and Central Avenue, across from New Orleans, in Jefferson Parish.

Elmwood

Fire again destroyed ELMWOOD on December 18, 1978, sparing only the original columns and brick interior and exterior walls. Plans to rebuild and reopen the restaurant are underway.

The original building was of the Creole raised-cottage design. A disastrous fire in 1940 left only the first story pillars intact, which were later incorporated into the building housing the famous Elmwood Restaurant.

ELMWOOD was probably constructed in 1762 by La Freniere, the revolutionary leader who led the attempted overthrow of Spanish rule. The land granted to him is still under the original title.

On River Road (La. 48), at Harahan, near the Huey P. Long Bridge, left on Evans Road to River Road, then turn left.

Destrehan Manor

Destrehan Manor

(OPEN TO PUBLIC)

DESTREHAN was built in 1787 by a free mulatto named Charles for Robert Antoine Robin de Logny. It was deeded to the River Road Historical Society by the American Oil Company.

The two wings are 1812 additions to the original building. The West Indies design of the roof is uncommon for plantation homes of this area. Referred to by local residents as "The Big House," DESTREHAN was built on land acquired by Jean Baptiste Destrehan in the 1700s.

The home was owned by many prominent people of various distinguished accomplishments. The visitor must surely feel a sense of history while viewing the house and grounds.

Open daily, 10-4; entrance fee; call (504) 764-9315.

On the River Road (La. 48), at Destrehan.

Ormond

Ormond

A typical two-story structure of brick below and wood above, this home dates back to the early 18th century. It was owned by the Butler family, and has been beautifully restored and landscaped. Private.

On the River Road (La. 48), one-and-a-half miles above Destrehan.

Amelina

Built well over a century ago, AMELINA was purchased from Zenon Bourdousquire by the Montegut family in 1852, which family has owned it since that date.

The home has hand-hewn timbers fastened with wooden dowels, and handmade iron hardware. Private.

On the River Road (La. 44), just south of LaPlace.

Woodland

A rambling one-story cottage, WOODLAND has a front window pane on which the following inscription appears: "Ann F. Hollingsworth, July 15, 1862." Private.

On the River Road (La. 44) and East 13th Street, Reserve.

San Francisco

(OPEN TO PUBLIC)

This magnificent structure, a longtime landmark along the Mississippi River, was built in 1854 by Edmond Bozonier Marmillion, and completed by his son Valsin. The house was originally named "San Frusquin" (one's all) by Valsin, because of the extensive amount of monies spent on the mansion. This great sweeping structure, teeming with scrolls, fluted pillars, rococo grillwork and galleries, is truly a showplace.

The architecture of the manor is French in design, but it is often called "Steamboat Gothic" and was the subject of a novel of the same name written by Frances Parkinson Keyes.

Marathon Oil Company now owns the property, which has been authentically restored to its original splendor.

Open to public daily, 10-4. Closed Christmas and New Year's Day. Large tours by appointment, call (504) 535-2341.

On La. 44, 35 miles upriver from New Orleans.

Hope

A simple one-story rambling cottage that dates back to the early 1800's, HOPE was owned by David Adams, from 1850 until the Civil War. Private.

On the River Road (La. 44) and Charles Street, Garyville.

San Francisco

Longview

Once the main house of a large plantation from which the town of Lutcher was subdivided, LONGVIEW was built by Joseph Gebelin who used the wood-over-adobe type of construction indicative of the era of Spanish occupation. It has been moved back from the river once. Private.

On the River Road (La. 44), just above the Lutcher Ferry.

Jefferson College

Here is a magnificent, elongated, three-story plantation house with 22 columns in an unbroken row across its main facade, and a triangular pediment above the central section.

This Greek Revival style structure was established in 1831 as a non-sectarian college for the higher education of the sons of wealthy Louisiana planters. It was state-supported for a few years until it closed. Bought by Valcour Aime, in 1859, it was reopened as Louisiana College. A new charter was obtained from the state in 1861.

During the War Between the States, it was used as a barracks by the Union forces. In 1864, Aime gave it to the Roman Catholic Marist Fathers who operated it as a boarding school for boys. Now it belongs to the Jesuit Order, and the property is its Manresa Retreat House for Laymen. Private. Grounds, however, are open to the public.

Only grounds open, Monday-Wednesday 9-4; after 3:30 Sunday.

On La. 44, two miles south of Convent.

"Uncle Sam" Plantation Site

This was one of the most efficient and spectacular plantation groups ever established in the United States. It had seven large buildings and 40 smaller ones. The largest of the seven was the main house, which was 100 feet square — not counting the broad galleries which surrounded it.

Centrally located among the remaining 46 buildings, the main house was a two-storied structure of plastered brick, with a hipped and dormered roof, supported on all sides by 28 giant Doric columns. It was reported that the main house cost $100,000 to build, and an additional $75,000 to furnish.

The buildings and plantation were demolished in 1940 to make way for the building of a levee, to prevent further land erosion by the river.

The plantation is said to have received its name from its builder, Samuel Fagot — who was called "Uncle Sam" by his relatives and friends.

A Freeport Sulphur Co. plant now stands on the site.

On La. 44, one-and-one-half miles north of Convent.

Colomb

Colomb House

A plantation home in miniature, COLOMB HOUSE is a variation of the Greek Revival style. One story high, two rooms wide, it has eight columns across the front, grouped in companionable twos. It was an architect's jewel whose most unusual feature was a complete room, with windows, rising above the roof. This room above the roof was used to house the boys of the family. Twin chimney stacks in balanced formation flank the one upper room. A gaily-covered coat-of-arms was put in plaster above the door.

It was built in 1835 by Christophe Colomb, Jr., an inventor, architect and engineer. One of his experiments was with clinkers formed during the burning of bagasse. Private.

On La. 44, four miles north of Convent.

Bagatelle

This one-and-a-half story, dormered home is believed to have been built in the 1800s for the daughter of Benjamin Tureaud of Union. The house may have been moved back to escape a changing river, but no definite records are available. A rounded glass in one of the windows is dated 1883. Private.

On the River Road (La. 44), three miles south of Longwood.

23

Tezcuco

Houmas House

Tezcuco

(OPEN TO PUBLIC)

TEZCUCO is located in the heart of the "Acadian Coast" — the land along the Mississippi in St. James and Ascension Parishes, site of the first large Acadian settlement in Louisiana. The house was completed in 1855 after five years of careful construction.

Built for Benjamin Tureaud, a veteran of the Mexican wars, it was named after a lake near Mexico City where Montezuma fled to escape the Spanish conquistador, Cortez.

The home is a large, raised "cottage" (in comparison to more elaborate and grander homes of the period), but it would hardly be considered such today. Its front bedrooms are 25 feet square and ceilings 15 feet high.

Among TEZCUCO's attractions are side galleries of lacy ironwork and a circular driveway.

Six miles west of I-10 on La. 44 (Old River Road); one mile north of Sunshine Bridge. Open Monday-Saturday, 10-4. Overnight accommodations available. Entrance fee. Call (504) 562-3929.

Houmas House

(OPEN TO PUBLIC)

This magnificent Greek Revival mansion was built by Col. John Smith Preston in 1840 on land originally owned by the Houmas Indians. In 1857 the plantation was sold to John Burnside, who became America's leading sugar planter.

It is one of the most imposing of Louisiana's fabled antebellum structures, two-and-one-half stories tall, with a parade of fourteen columns on three sides, dormers against the sky and a glass-windowed belvedere as a crown. Hexagonal garçonnieres are at either side, and the early four-room 18th century house at the rear is connected to the main house, forming a carriageway. It is surrounded by live oaks, magnolias and formal gardens and is furnished with antiques of the period. The heirs of the late Dr. George Crozat, who accomplished this superb restoration, are the present owners. "Hush, Hush, Sweet Charlotte" was filmed here.

On display is a rare copy of the 1931 Pelican edition of the famous 1858 Persac Map of the Plantations of the Mississippi. This is Pelican's oldest item still in print. The current edition is available in the gift shop.

Open February through October, 10-5; November through January, 10-4; closed Thanksgiving, Christmas, and New Year's Day. Nominal entrance fee.

Accessible via Interstate 10 (Burnside exit), on River Road (La. 942), at Burnside.

Bocage

Bocage

This two-story home of characteristic brick construction below and wood above is square in appearance and classic in design. Across the front gallery is an odd design utilizing wooden pillars; the outer six are thick and heavy, and the middle pair are thin and light in contrast.

At the back of the house is a partly-enclosed gallery which extends to both floors. A heavy entablature hides the roof.

This finely-ornamented gem was built in 1801 by Marius Pons Bringier as a wedding present for his 15-year-old daughter, Francoise, and Christophe Colomb — a Parisian who claimed kinship with Christopher Columbus.

BOCAGE — which means "Shady Retreat" in French— was extensively repaired in 1840, and became one of the showplaces along the Mississippi just before and after the War Between the States.

Private.

On Hwy. 942, two miles above Burnside.

l'Hermitage

l'Hermitage

With original walls of brick-between-posts surrounded by Doric columns, THE HERMITAGE was a splendid mansion in Greek Revival style. Two dormer windows break the roof, and an inner gallery on the second floor does not detract from its overall massive simplicity.

It was built in 1812 by Marius Pons Bringier as a wedding gift for his son, Michel Douradou. It is the earliest surviving Greek Revival style plantation home remaining in Louisiana.

The Bringier men were among the Creoles who fought under Jackson at the Battle of New Orleans, and Douradou named his home THE HERMITAGE after the Tennessee home of his hero. Group tours by appointment, call (504) 891-8493; luncheon facilities available to such groups in a restored outbuilding on the grounds.

On the River Road (La. 942), one mile below Darrow.

Proceed along La. 75 at Darrow.

Ashland-Belle Helene

Ashland - Belle Helene

(OPEN TO PUBLIC)

A huge house of unusual height, ASHLAND is surrounded by a colonnade of pillars, eight to a side, and set in a horseshoe of live oak trees. The ground floor gallery is paved in tile and brick, and galleries extend nearly 20 feet on each side.

Built in 1841 by Duncan Kenner, Confederate minister plenipotentiary to France, and designed by James Gallier, of New Orleans, ASHLAND was one of the great sugar plantations. Kenner named it after Henry Clay's home.

The plantation later was bought by John Reuss and renamed BELLE HELENE after his granddaughter, Hélène.

"Beguiled," starring Clint Eastwood and Geraldine Page, was filmed here in 1970.

Scenes for Warner Brothers' motion picture, "Band of Angels," starring Clark Gable, were made here in 1957.

Open daily 9-4; nominal entrance fee.

Off La. 75 on the Old River Road; six miles above Darrow.

Indian Camp

The house is of white brick with heavy columns and dates from the late 1850's. It is now the administration building of the U. S. Public Health Service Hospital, only institution of its kind in the United States. Private.

On La. 75, at Carville.

Home Place

Built in the days of the Spanish occupation, HOME PLACE is of typical early Louisiana Colonial construction — **briquette entre poteaux,** or brick-between-posts.

It is presently occupied by descendants of the original owners, and has been moved back to avoid destruction by the river. Private.

On the River Road (La. 75), at St. Gabriel.

Longwood

Also built during the Spanish occupation, LONGWOOD is a cypress building with a hipped roof, supported by slender wooden columns. Both of its galleries have iron railings.

The back part of the house was added to the present structure in 1835. Private.

On the River Road (La. 75), 10 miles south of Baton Rouge.

LSU Rural Life Museum

(OPEN TO PUBLIC)

Located on the Burden Research Plantation, a 450-acre agricultural research experiment station owned by Louisiana State University, the Rural Life Museum preserves an important part of the state's heritage.

Conceived and developed by Steele and Ione Burden and Cecil G. Taylor, former chancellor at LSU in Baton Rouge, the museum encompasses five acres, 15 buildings and hundreds of artifacts reflecting plantation life in 18th and 19th century Louisiana. Some of the buildings are original period structures, along with authentic tools, household utensils, furniture, and farm implements.

The Museum is divided into three areas: the Barn, containing artifacts dating from prehistoric times to the early 20th century; the Working Plantation, a complex of authentically furnished plantation buildings; and Louisiana Folk Architecture, portrayed in six buildings and illustrating the various cultures of Louisiana settlers.

Open 8:30 a.m. to 4 p.m. Monday through Friday, except during LSU holidays. Groups must schedule tours one month in advance; children under 12 not admitted. No admission fee. Telephone (504) 766-8241.

Located off Essen Lane, just south of the I-10 intersection in Baton Rouge.

Mount Hope Plantation

(OPEN TO PUBLIC)

Built on a Spanish land grant obtained in 1786, MOUNT HOPE was constructed in 1817 by Joseph Sharp, a German planter. It is beautifully furnished in the Federal, Sheraton and Empire periods. The twelve-and-a-half-foot ceilings are typical of the early Southern planter's home.

This imposing home served as an encampment to Confederate troops during the War Between the States.

Listed in the National Register of Historic Places.

Open daily, 9-5; entrance fee. Overnight accommodations and banquet facilities available. Call (504) 766-8600.

At 8151 Highland Road in Baton Rouge.

Magnolia Mound

(OPEN TO PUBLIC)

This home, built in the late 1700's, has a front porch 80 feet across. It was once the home of Prince Achille Murat, son of Charles Louis Napoleon Achille Murat — nephew of Bonaparte and Crown Prince of Naples.

The house took its name from the grove of trees in which it was set, and was built on a bluff, or mound, overlooking the Mississippi.

The structure is not much different from what it looked like 140 years ago. Wide, single-storied and built almost five feet off the ground, the house boasted beautiful hand-carved woodwork and thick plank floors—both of which are still in splendid shape.

Open Tuesday-Sunday 10-4; entrance fee.

At 2161 Nicholson Drive in Baton Rouge.

Stewart-Dougherty House

This imposing two-story home was built for Nathan Knox by Nelson Potts in 1854. Massive square plastered-brick columns support a hipped roof and second floor gallery.

Shortly afterward, Mrs. Nolan Stewart, daughter of James McCalop, a pioneer landowner of the area, purchased the home. It has been maintained by her descendants since that time.

During the War Between the States it was used as a U. S. General Hospital, 1862-63. Private.

At 741 North Street in Baton Rouge.

Potts House

Potts House

This two-story brick townhouse was built in 1846 by Nelson Potts, formerly of New Jersey. Potts, an accomplished brick mason, had come to Baton Rouge and established a brickyard on the outskirts of town. It is likely that he built this house, at the edge of the brickyard, as an example of his handicraft, as well as his family's home. Private.

At 831 North Street in Baton Rouge.

Goodwood

This white, cement-covered brick home was built in 1856 by Dr. S. G. Laycock, on land which was granted to Thomas Hutchings by George III in 1776.

It has broad, iron-railed galleries supported by four Doric columns across the front. GOODWOOD had running water piped to washstands in all rooms — which was an unusual feature for a plantation home. Private.

At 7307 Goodwood Avenue at Lobdell, in Baton Rouge.

31

TOUR 4

Monte Vista

Built in the 1850's by Louis Favrot, MONTE VISTA has six square plastered columns which support the gallery and the roof.

The building was restored in 1916 by Horace Wilkinson, Jr., and contains many family heirlooms — one of which is a massive gold watch owned by George Washington. Private.

On the River Road (La. 1), West Bank, one mile south of the Mississippi River Bridge, across from Baton Rouge.

Sand Bar

This home was built in 1850 by Captain Vaughn, of Virginia, who named it for a sand bar in the river at that point. It is now owned by the Dameron Family. Private.

On the River Road (La. 1), above Brusly.

Antonio

An example of a simple country home, ANTONIO dates back to about 1800, and is typical of the construction of that period. Private.

On the River Road (La. 1), just above Brusly.

Cazenave

The front part of this house is approximately 125 years old. The back wing was added more recently, and is part of the old Caire store — purchased when the river threatened it. Private.

Off the River Road (La. 1), at Brusly.

St. Basil's

(OPEN TO PUBLIC)

This beautiful Greek Revival mansion was built in 1850 and became St. Basil's Academy in 1859.

Today the antebellum home is open to the public as a restaurant, the splendor of the interior to be enjoyed by the diner.

Restaurant is open Monday-Friday, 11-10; Saturday, 5-10; and Sunday, 11-3.

Overnight accommodations available. Call (504) 687-7661.

On La. 1, North at Court Street in Plaquemine.

St. Louis

ST. LOUIS is a tall, white building in the Greek Revival style, with six Ionic columns supporting the first gallery and six of the more ornate Corinthian style on the second floor. A belvedere atop the roof afforded a sweeping view of the river, and rich cast-iron work gave it Creole character. An unusual feature of a South Louisiana home was the cellar.

It was built in 1858 of cypress with shutters of green trim by Edward J. Gay, of St. Louis, who named it after that city.

The plantation was originally known as Home Plantation when established by Capt. Joseph Erwin in 1807. Private.

On La. 405, two miles below Plaquemine.

Tallyho

Once assigned as the overseer's home, this building was later taken over by the owners when the main house burned. TALLYHO has been in the same family for over a century. Private.

On the River Road (La. 405), one-half mile south of Bayou Goula.

Nottoway

NOTTOWAY is the largest plantation home in the South. The three-story mansion contains 64 rooms and was considered immense even by the standards of the Golden Age period.

Henry Howard, a New Orleans architect, was commissioned by John H. Randolph to build this most palatial residence. Completed in 1859, NOTTOWAY, named for the county of Mr. Randolph's birth in Virginia, was a self-sufficient 7,000 acre sugarcane plantation.

The interior features elaborate wood carvings and plaster work with eleven foot doors and fifteen-and-a-half-foot ceilings, blending Greek Revival and Italianate architectural styles. The home has been completely restored and displays beautiful period furnishings.

Listed in the National Register of Historic Places.

Open daily, 9-5; entrance fee; restaurant open daily, 11-3; overnight accommodations available with advance reservations.

On La. 1 (River Road) two miles north of White Castle.

Mulberry Grove

This two-and-a-half-story antebellum home, built in 1836 by Dr. Duffel, has been beautifully restored. Private.

On the River Road (La. 405), seven miles below White Castle.

Lafitte's Landing

(OPEN TO PUBLIC)

This raised Acadian cottage, which dates from 1797, has been completely restored as a restaurant. It is reputed to have been the home of Jean Lafitte, the pirate, from 1799 to 1804. The architecture of the building is typical of the period. The solid mahogany bar was built in New Orleans around 1800.

Open Monday, 11-3; Tuesday-Saturday, 11-3, 6-10; Sunday, 11-8.

On Sunshine Bridge access road, west bank of the Mississippi River, Donaldsonville.

Valcour Aime Plantation Site

This splendid mansion, which burned about 1920, rivalled VERSAILLES as the most opulent plantation home in a state once dotted with elegant residences. Originally constructed in the late 1700s by Don Francisco Aime, it was inherited by Valcour Aime at a young age, and he set about to rebuild it in the grandest manner.

He added extensive rear wings to form a court paved with black and white marble. An elaborately carved marble stairway replaced the original mahogany one. Marble hallways graced the lower floor and marble statuary could be found throughout the grounds. The main building contained eight huge rooms, with four others on each floor in each wing.

Marble mantels, crystal chandeliers and immense pier mirrors with gold leaf frames gave the mansion's interior a splendor that seldom has been equalled. It is marked by a historical marker.

Off La. 18, near OAK ALLEY.

Oak Alley

Oak Alley

(OPEN TO PUBLIC)

Magnificent OAK ALLEY is in the Greek Revival style of plastered brick, 70 feet square, girded by 28 Doric columns each eight feet in circumference.

The famed oak alley, a double row of live oaks, 14 to a side, leads to the River Road some 300 yards distant. The trees range from 15 to 29 feet in circumference and their branches have long since interlaced, forming a leafy canopy from the road to the house. Spacing between the trees is exactly 80 feet.

The home was left by Josephine Stewart as a nonprofit foundation so that others might continue to enjoy her beauty and dream of her rich past.

Built 1830-39 by Jacques Telepher Roman III, brother of Andre Roman, twice-governor of Louisiana, it was originally named Bon Sejour. Later the name was changed because of the interest in the avenue of oaks. The first successful attempt at grafting pecans was performed here in 1846 by a slave gardener.

The name OAK ALLEY was given to it by steamboat passengers when they saw the line of trees with the pink house at the end. It is believed that the trees were planted by an early unknown French settler who may have built a primitive home here in 1690.

Open daily, 9-5:30, March through October; 9-5, November through February; closed Thanksgiving, Christmas, and New Year's Day. Nominal entrance fees. Restaurant open daily 11-3.

On River Road, near Vacherie.

St. Joseph

The house, of **briquette entre poteaux** construction (moss and clay between cypress columns, under weatherboard walls), was built about 1820 by a Dr. Mericq. It was purchased from him by Valcour Aime as a wedding present for his daughter, Josephine.

Ten large brick columns rise from the ground floor to the gallery; ten square wooden columns rise from the brick ones to the steep, hipped roof. Private.

On the River Road (La. 18), two-and-one-half miles west of Vacherie.

Felicity

This home was built by Valcour Aime as a wedding present for another daughter about 1850. It has six large, square wooden pillars and a single dormer in its low slanting roof; it also boasts red Italian marble mantels. Private.

On the River Road (La. 18), one-and-one-half miles west of Vacherie.

Waguespack

According to the local history, WAGUESPACK was used as a hospital during the War Between the States. Private.

On the River Road (La. 18), just east of Vacherie.

Hymel

This two-and-one-half-story home, once owned by the Legendres, is typical of the "country home" construction of the era. Private.

On the River Road (La. 18), just west of the Vacherie Ferry.

Whitney Plantation House

Also an example of the moss-mud-cypress construction, WHITNEY was built about 1840 and is a raised cottage with wide galleries at the front and rear, supported by square wooden pillars.

The hinges, bolts and other hardware were handmade by slaves. Private.

On the River Road (La. 18), between Vacherie and Edgard.

Evergreen Plantation House

This two-story brick structure was built about 1840 by Ralph Brou in the Greek Revival style. Tall, massive stucco and brick columns support the roof and wide galleries. The hipped roof is broken by dormer windows and topped by a balustrade. A curving exterior stair mounts to the portico of the second floor.

To the rear is a complete group of buildings, including pigeonniers, servants' quarters and barns. Even the privies, which the French called "Louis XIV's," were of brick and of the same classic Greek Temple design. Large magnolias may be seen, and a fine avenue of live oaks, 39 to a side and 40 feet apart, leads away from the river.

One of the finest examples of a Louisiana planter's house of more than a century ago, the plans and dimensions of EVERGREEN are now in the Federal Archives at Washington. Private.

On the River Road (La. 18), five miles west of Edgard.

Evergreen

Haydel-Jones House

This home was constructed in the 1830's with interior doors which were handmade from planks by slave carpenters. Private.

On the River Road (La. 18), lower Edgard.

Goldmine

Dating back to the middle 1800's, this home has been owned by Thomas May, Octave Hymel, F. E. Tassin and the Champagnes, among others. Private.

On the River Road (La. 18), below Edgard.

Glendale Plantation House

The foundation for this building was laid about 1807, and the building itself was completed a few years later. The house is a two-story, cement-covered brick structure with eight square wooden pillars.

The timbers are hand-hewn and fastened with wooden pegs; the hardware and elaborate mantels were handmade on the plantation. Private.

On the River Road (La. 18), one-and-a-half miles below Lucy.

Keller House

Built for the Fortier family about 1801, this structure has typical French-Spanish architectural design — and features a one-inch-thick white plaster veneer on its walls. The plantation was part of a Spanish land grant given to an ancestor of the family.

It was later purchased by the Kellers, after whom it was renamed; and was also known as Home Place during the Kellers' occupancy. Private.

On the River Road (La. 18), one-half mile above Hahnville.

Magnolia Lane

(OPEN BY APPOINTMENT)

Of West Indies design, this home was built on the original Old Spanish Trail, at that time the only wagon road from the West into New Orleans.

Edward Fortier built MAGNOLIA LANE in 1784, on land which he received in a Spanish grant. The plantation is historically noted as the land on which Francis Quinette, of St. Louis, grew the first strawberries in Louisiana.

Located across the levee from the house, 600 yards to the north, is the site of Fort Banks.

Open by appointment only, 9-5; closed Monday and Tuesday. Call (504) 347-1323 for reservations. Entrance fee.

On the River Road (La. 18), at Nine Mile Point, above Westwego, one mile north of the Huey P. Long Bridge.

Derbigny

(OPEN TO PUBLIC)

This lovely old home, a Louisiana raised cottage typical of the period, was built by Charles Derbigny in the 1830s and named for his father, Pierre, fifth governor of Louisiana. It was originally a 1500-acre sugarcane plantation.

In 1947 the Collenberg family purchased the home and grounds. The Collenbergs now operate a Hunt Club and Nursery on the lovely grounds with live oaks, pecans, and magnolias. Bring a picnic lunch to enjoy by the pond on the only working plantation in the greater New Orleans area.

Open to the public Tuesday through Sunday, 10-5. Entrance fee.

On River Road (La. 541), near Oak Avenue above Westwego.

Derbigny

Tchoupitoulas Plantation
Restaurant

(OPEN TO PUBLIC)

This 19th century plantation, turned into a restaurant, features Creole cooking for luncheon and dinner. The flavor of the Old South permeates the house and grounds to delight the visitor.

Open seven days a week; call (504) 436-1277 for reservations and for hours open each day for lunch and dinner.

La. 18 near Avondale, 3¼ miles from Huey P. Long Bridge, West Bank.

TOUR 5

Rosella

Built in 1814, this plantation home has been recently restored to its original beauty. It has been owned by the same family ever since it was established. Private.

On the River Road (La. 308), East Bank, above Raceland.

Acadia

The plantation site on which this house is located is reputed to have been established by Jim Bowie on advice of Jean Lafitte.

The present ACADIA HOUSE was built about 1842 by Phillip Key — relative of Francis Scott Key, composer of "The Star Spangled Banner." Set in a grove of live oaks, ACADIA is a rambling, yellow, one-story wooden cottage with ornate gables and dormers, and is now owned by the Plater family. Private.

On the River Road (La. 1), West Bank, two miles south of Thibodaux.

Chatchie

Boasting weatherboards of hand-shaped cypress, CHAT-CHIE is a two-story cottage of early Louisiana Colonial construction. Among its many features is one of the first six pianos ever built in America. Private.

On the River Road (La. 308), East Bank, four miles south of Thibodaux.

Rienzi

Rienzi

An Old World design is "Spanish style" RIENZI, with its twin stairways curving gracefully from the entrance. It has a paved lower porch and a gallery that encircles the house. It is of cypress, cedar and brick. The trees above the roof are hung with Spanish moss. It was named after Cola di Rienzi, a 14th century Italian patriot.

It was built in 1796, reportedly as a retreat for Queen Maria Louisa of Spain in event of defeat in the Napoleonic Wars. Juan Ygnacia de Egana, believed to be the builder, obtained title to RIENZI and lived there for nearly half a century following the sale of Louisiana to the United States. Private.

On La. 308, near Thibodaux.

Madewood

Madewood

(OPEN TO PUBLIC)

One of the best-preserved plantation homes of the ante-bellum period is MADEWOOD, whose name comes from the fact that its cypress timbers were hand-carved from trees on the 3,000-acre plantation. It follows the Greek Revival tradition, having its columns resting on the stylobate, or continuous pavement, instead of individual pedestals. Its 25-foot ceilings, large central halls, spacious ballroom, carved winding walnut staircase and more than 20 rooms indicate its magnificence. It is a large two-story house of stucco-covered brick set on a low terrace.

The house, grounds, carriage house and family cemetery are now on the tour. MADEWOOD is embellished with many fine works of art from the collection of its owners.

Begun in 1840 and completed eight years later, MADEWOOD was the home of Colonel Thomas Pugh of North Carolina. He died of yellow fever before it was finished. Six Ionic columns support the great roof. On either side of the main structure are connecting wings that duplicate its architectural theme. Its interior is dominated by a massive entrance hallway with Corinthian columns.

Additional historic structures have been moved to the grounds, forming a complex of important buildings from the bayou area: the Elmfield slave cottage, indigenous to the region; the Marshall-Charlet House, circa 1822, which was built by riverboat Captain Pierre Charlet in Plattenville and moved across six miles of cane fields to MADEWOOD; and Marquette, an Acadian cottage, originally the blacksmith's home in Napoleonville. The Rosedale plantation home was moved recently, and plans for restoration are to convert Rosedale into a theatre for future cultural performances.

Open daily 10-5.

On La. 308, two miles south of Napoleonville.

Belle Alliance

This is an elaborate home with a tall basement, out-sweeping stairs and ironwork on the balcony and side porches. Six square, two-story wooden columns support the roof.

BELLE ALLIANCE differs from neighboring mansions in its structure, which combined the classic revival of the 1830's with the airiness that distinguishes the New Orleans French Quarter. Its 33 rooms are strikingly furnished in the Victorian period. The main wing has 24 rooms.

Built in 1846 by Charles Kock, a Belgian aristocrat, it was the home of that family until 1915. It had 7,000 acres, mostly in sugar cane. The Kock garden was noted for its magnificent camellias. Crumbling brick piles mark the BELLE ALLIANCE sugar house, once one of the most important west of the Mississippi. Private.

The plantation today is 4,300 acres of cane land along Bayou Lafourche, five miles from Donaldsonville, on La. 308. Enter Donaldsonville. Junction with La. 1, south, for Tour 6.

Belle Alliance

TOUR 6

St. Emma

This plantation site was once operated in conjunction with BELLE ALLIANCE, which is just across the Bayou. Private.

On La. 1, about four miles south of Donaldsonville.

Creole

CREOLE was built in the early 1800's by Emeron Landry. The Land was deeded to the ancestors of the present owners by a Spanish grant. Private.

On La. 1, three miles north of Paincourtville.

Edward Douglass White Memorial

(OPEN TO PUBLIC)

This old plantation home is an example of the earliest type of Louisiana plantation home — the "raised cottage type" — so popular in the late 18th century. It was built of hand-hewn cypress timber, put together with wooden pegs and elevated on tall brick pillars; it also has a brick basement.

It was built about 1790 by Edward Douglass White, Sr.,

who was judge of the Lafourche Interior Territory, governor of Louisiana from 1835-1839 and a member of the U. S. Senate. The home was the birthplace of Edward Douglass White, Jr., the state's most famous jurist. He served on the Louisiana Supreme Court, as a member of the U.S. Senate and as an associate justice of the U.S. Supreme Court for 16 years. He later served as Chief Justice for 11 years.

The 1,600-acre plantation was purchased by the government in 1936, and is now a memorial museum, controlled by the Louisiana State Parks and Recreation Commission.

A nominal fee is charged for adults and students; children under six, free.

Museum open Wednesday through Sunday, 9-5. Closed Christmas and New Year's Day.

On La. 1, five miles north of Thibodaux.

Edward Douglass White Memorial

Armitage

Built in 1852, ARMITAGE stands as one of the finest examples of plantation home restoration. The present owners, Mr. and Mrs. Frank Wurzlow, acquired the home in 1948 and began restoration in 1961, which is now complete. The front of the house remains essentially as it was orig-

46

inally, although three dormers have been added to light the upper rooms.

One unusual feature is the size of the closets—one 50 feet long and another 18 feet long. Private.

Located three miles south of Thibodaux on La. 20.

Ducros

Built just prior to the Civil War on a Spanish land grant, this plantation home reportedly was modeled after the "Hermitage," Andrew Jackson's Nashville home. A two-story wooden house, it has eight tall square columns supporting wide galleries. A wing was later added to the house on either side.

The house and plantation were purchased in 1846 by Colonel Van Winder, who developed the land into the first great sugar cane plantation in Terrebonne Parish. Confederate and Union soldiers occupied the house during the Civil War. Private.

On La. 24, ½ mile north of Schriever.

Sonnier

This plantation home was built in the early 1800's by John G. Potts, and is an example of early Louisiana Colonial construction. Private.

On La. 24, three miles south of Schriever.

Magnolia

Built in 1854, this two-story building was built by Thomas Ellis and stands among the flowering trees from which it takes its name.

During the War Between the States, MAGNOLIA was used as a hospital by Federal troops.

William A. Shaffer bought the place in 1874 and completed the structure as it stands today. Private.

On La. 311, three miles south of Schriever.

Ardoyne

Ardoyne

ARDOYNE, a Scottish word meaning "knoll," is one of the few homes of architectural significance that was copied from a picture. Begun in 1897 and completed in 1900, the structure was built to resemble a picture of a Scottish castle that the owner, John D. Shaffer, had seen in a magazine.

Notable features of the home include its dominantly cypress construction and gingerbread trim. The ceiling and stairway of the center hall are highlighted by inlaid wood. Private. Tours can be arranged by calling (504) 872-3197. Located eight miles northwest of Houma on La. 311.

Listed in the National Register of Historic Places.

On La. 311, eight miles north of Houma.

Ellendale

This lovely moss-draped home, built during the early 1800s, was acquired by Andrew McCollam in 1851 and has remained in the McCollam family since that time. Named for Andrew McCollam's wife Ellen, the house contains many treasured family heirlooms.

Since its original construction, the house has been enlarged several times. On the grounds still stands an old brick sugar house, a reminder of activities of bygone days.

On La. 311, seven miles north of Houma.

Crescent Plantation

William A. Shaffer established this plantation in the early 19th century.

The creole raised cottage, which dates from 1849, is a typical structure of the period with square wooden columns, wide gallery, shutters and dormer windows. Private.

On La. 311, three-and-a-half miles north of Houma.

Southdown Plantation/Terrebonne Museum

(OPEN TO PUBLIC)

This English manor house was started in 1858 by William Minor. The second story was added by his son, Henry C. Minor, in 1893. The home has 20 rooms, flanked by 2 turrets. The restoration of the home and museum was started in 1977 by the Terrebonne Historical and Cultural Society, to whom the structure now belongs.

The museum contains a collection of Boehm and Doughty porcelain birds, Senator Allen Ellender's memorabilia and original furniture from the Minor family. Stained glass scenes of sugarcane and magnolia blossoms grace the hallway doors.

Listed in the National Register of Historic Places.

Tours daily, except legal holidays, from 10-3:30. Entrance fee. Call (504) 851-0154.

In Houma, on La. 311, one-fourth mile north of Lafayette St.

Orange Grove

Dating from the 1840s ORANGE GROVE is an outstanding example of the solid building construction of the period. It has been restored to its original beauty. Preserved were the *briquette-entre-poteau* (brick between posts) construction, *faux bois* (false wood) treatment of the doors and other features when the present owners lovingly researched and restored this one-and-a-half-story home.

On the banks of Bayou Black, the historian is reminded that when the home was built, the waterways of Terrebonne Parish were the means of transportation for area residents. Private.

Listed in the National Register of Historic Places.

On U. S. 90, 12 miles west of Houma. Enter Houma; junction with U. S. 90, west, for Tour 7.

TOUR 7

Joshua B. Cary House

(OPEN TO PUBLIC)

This beautiful antebellum Greek Revival mansion, which dates from 1839, has been restored to its original splendor.

The home was built by Joshua B. Cary for his bride, Eleanor Gordy. The entire exterior is of cypress, an enduring wood found in many early homes. The interior was constructed with pegs, notches and square nails.

Open to the public daily. Call (318) 836-5598. Entrance fee.

At intersection of La. 317 and La. 182 in Centerville.

Bocage

This beautiful restoration of what once was OAK-BLUFF PLANTATION HOME was transported seven miles by barge to its present site on Bayou Teche. The home of the E. H. Sutters, Bocage is believed to be the largest structure ever transferred in this manner.

The two-and-one-half story home was built some time after 1846, when the sugar cane plantation on which it originally stood became the property of the ancestors of Mrs. Fairfax Foster Sutter. The Greek Revival structure stands in a beautiful setting of oaks on Bayou Teche and is an outstanding example of Louisiana antebellum homes. Private.

On La. 182, five miles east of Franklin.

Frances

(OPEN TO PUBLIC)

This lovely restored home—more than 160 years old—is one of the oldest homes along Bayou Teche. An antique and interior design shop is housed within this Louisiana colonial style mansion.

Open 9-5; closed Sunday and Monday except by appointment. Call (318) 828-5472.

On La. 182, four miles east of Franklin.

50

Dixie

Constructed of cypress both inside and out, DIXIE was built by the Wilkes family in 1850. It is a two-story structure, with a hipped roof and four square columns supporting a pedimented portico.

It was purchased by Murphy J. Foster, former Louisiana governor and U.S. Senator, in 1886. Private.

On La. 182, one-and-a-half miles east of Franklin.

Arlington

(OPEN TO PUBLIC)

This beautiful plantation home was built about 1855 by Euphrazie Carlin, a wealthy planter who owned about 2,000 slaves.

The home is a large white wooden building set back in a deep lawn amid magnolia, palm and evergreen trees. Its pedimented portico has four fluted Corinthian columns, also of wood, which are repeated in a modified form on the side porches. The upper and lower balconies on both the front and sides of the home are decorated with wrought-iron balustrades.

Open Tuesday-Saturday, 10-4; entrance fee.

On La. 182, on eastern outskirts of Franklin.

O'Niell Home

This one-and-a-half story cottage was constructed about 1851 by Thomas J. Foster, father of Louisiana Governor Murphy J. Foster, on a lot which once was part of a large plantation owned by Simon Mathison. The property was acquired in 1873 by Franklin mayor Wilson McKerall, Jr., and sold to his son-in-law, John O'Niell, in 1895.

Although considered to be cottage architecture, the house is particularly spacious and is topped by a gabled roof, presenting an inviting appearance in uncluttered lines of exterior white with green shutters. Private.

At 201 Main Street in Franklin.

Fleming House

Like the O'NIELL HOME next door, FLEMING HOUSE stands on what once was the Mathison estate. Constructed about 1889, FLEMING HOUSE features four square columns supporting the galleries, which are enclosed by a railing of intricate design.

The two-story front section drops at the rear to one level, part of which was added in later years. Once known as the MAHON HOME, after the family who resided in it for some 60 years, the house now bears the name of its present owners, Judge and Mrs. Robert Fleming. Private.

At 203 Main Street in Franklin.

Eaglesfield

This was the principal dwelling on a plantation purchased in 1859 by Dr. James Fontaine from Hiram Anderson. Dr. Fontaine then sold 12 of its 100 arpents to the Rev. Dunn for use as the site of Rugby School.

Subsequent owners include Euphroisie Carlin, Thomas Eaglesfield, R. E. Milling and Mrs. Minnie Hanson Connolly. It was donated to the Catholic Church in 1920 by Mrs. Connolly and is now used as a chapel and classrooms.

Behind Hanson School on Anderson Street in Franklin.

Grevemberg House

(OPEN TO PUBLIC)

Built in 1851 by Henry C. Wilson, this white two-story frame house has four slender Corinthian columns and an upper balcony edged with a balustrade of delicate wooden spindles.

A diamond-shaped window with green shutters is set in the center of the gabled roof. Restored by the St. Mary Parish Landmarks Society, it houses the St. Mary Parish Museum.

Open Thursday-Sunday, 10-4.

On Sterling Road, east of Franklin.

Oaklawn Manor

Oaklawn Manor

(OPEN TO PUBLIC)

This Greek Colonial Manor House was built in the early eighteen hundreds by Alexander Porter, an Irishman, who was one of the founders of the State of Louisiana. First a member of the commission that drew up the new State's constitution, he went on to be an Associate Justice of the first Louisiana Supreme Court, a U. S. Senator and was the founder of the Whig Party in Louisiana.

Captain Clyde A. Barbour, who restored the mansion in 1927, collected the rare antique furnishings in Europe. They are of the period when the Manor was built.

The grounds contain a magnificent collection of Live Oaks said to have been growing at Oaklawn when Columbus discovered America and called the largest grove in the nation.

The gardens were landscaped by a French landscape architect and here is found a Cedar Walk, unique in America, formed by a double row of cedars brought by Judge Porter from Tennessee.

For many years a daughter of Captain and Mrs. Barbour and her husband, Mr. and Mrs. Thomas J. Holmes, II preserved the beautiful place and it was visited by many from near and far.

In 1963 Mr. and Mrs. George B. Thomson completely renovated the manor house and extensive grounds to perpetuate this elegant example of Louisiana's heritage.

Open to the public, 10-4; entrance fee.

Facing Bayou Teche, on Irish Bend Road, northwest of Franklin.

Darby

Reputedly built about 1765, this home has been renovated to house a branch of the St. Mary Bank and Trust Co.

On La. 182 in Baldwin.

Heaton

Built by Albert Heaton in 1853 on a site bordering the Franklin cemetery, this small Italian villa was moved by barge some 15 miles up Bayou Teche to Linwood, near Charenton, in 1966. Designed by Alexander Davis, an important 19th century architect, the house is of board and batten construction, with a center section rising to a second floor. Private.

Three miles north of Baldwin on La. 326.

Albania Plantation House

(OPEN BY APPOINTMENT)
Set in a lovely grove of live oaks, this large, white home has six square wooden columns across the south side and three dormer windows along its gabled roof. This was the carriage entrance to the home in 1842. The main front of house faces the Bayou Teche to the north.

Charles François Grevemberg was the founder of AL-BANIA. General Nathaniel Banks occupied it after the Battle of Berwick Bay. An anchor from the scuttled gunboat "Queen of the West" is on display on the grounds.

ALBANIA construction began in 1837 and was completed in 1842. Cypress from the plantation was used to build the house. Red clay from the bayou banks was used to make the bricks for the foundation. Slave labor built the home, with the exception of the spiral stair curving to the third story, which was imported from France.

ALBANIA MANSION is now owned by Emily Cyr Bridges and is kept in splendid condition. It is truly one of the finer Louisiana plantation homes.

A unique attraction is the Doll Room, where a renowned collection is on display. The Napoleon Room has a seven-piece set of Directoire furniture. The French Room has Louis XV and Louis XVI furnishings. There are many pieces of Mallard and Signourette furniture throughout the house.

Open by appointment only. Entrance fee. Guest cottage available. Call (318) 276-4816.

On U. S. 90, ¼ mile east of Jeanerette.

Albania

Enterprise Plantation House

Built in the 1830's by the Patout family, ENTERPRISE is one of the oldest sugar plantations and mills still in operation by the descendants of the original owners.

The Patout family was given a Royal French grant to establish a wine industry here, but found the soil was not of the proper type for wine grapes. The plantation branched into sugar planting and became very successful. Private.

Off La. 85, behind the Sugar House, at Patoutville.

Bayside

This is a two-story, whitewashed brick building in the Greek Revival style, with six plastered-brick Doric columns and decorative wooden balustrades, surrounded by a grove of oaks.

Built in 1850 by Francis D. Richardson, a member of the Louisiana Legislature prior to the War Between the States, and classmate and friend of Edgar Allen Poe, BAYSIDE is sometimes called the "Old Sanders Place," because of a later owner. Private.

On Hwy. 87, one mile west of Jeanerette.

Alice

Built around 1800 and recently transported down Bayou Teche to Alice Plantation near Jeanerette, this is an excellent example of Louisiana Colonial architecture. Its highlights include round plastered columns, hand-made brick lower story and wooden upper story. Private.

Two miles west of Jeanerette.

Fuselier

Agricole Fuselier II built this home about 1803, modeling it after the DARBY HOUSE, listed above. Private.

On Charenton Road (La. 326), one-half mile east of Baldwin.

Beau Pré

This beautiful plantation home was built in 1830 by John W. Jeanerette, after whom the city of Jeanerette was named.

A guest in the home was Longfellow, and it was here he was inspired to write his famous "Evangeline." The home also served as the government house. Private.

On Hwy. 182, five miles northwest of Jeanerette.

Joseph Jefferson Home

(GARDENS ONLY OPEN TO PUBLIC)

Built in 1870 by Joseph Jefferson, the world-famous 19th century actor who discovered rock salt on Jefferson Island, this unique structure was made of native cypress cut on the Island. The original design reflects the influence of Jefferson's travels, combining Spanish, Gothic and Southern styles of architecture. French craftsmen were brought from New Orleans for its construction.

Jefferson won world acclaim by his portrayal of the title role in Washington Irving's "Rip Van Winkle." President Grover Cleveland was among the celebrities who visited Jefferson here.

The homesite is also noted for its fabulous Rip Van Winkle's Live Oak Gardens, fittingly named for a character Jefferson played on the stage. Begun by J. L. Bayless, Jr., following World War II, the 20-acre gardens today offer an enchanting experience throughout the four seasons.

The Rip Van Winkle Gardens, opened by J. L. Bayless, Jr., following World War II, were demolished in a natural disaster in 1981. Private.

On Highways 675 and 14, seven miles southwest of New Iberia.

The Shadows-on-the-Teche

(OPEN TO PUBLIC)

The-Shadows-on-the-Teche is one of the Deep South's most fabled houses. It was built in 1831-1834 for David Weeks, a wealthy planter, on the banks of the Bayou Teche. The late Weeks Hall, descendant of the builder and a noted Louisiana artist, began restoration of the house in 1922. During Weeks Hall's lifetime, numerous celebrities, attracted by his exceptional personality and the mysterious charm of his home, were entertained at the Shadows. In 1958 Weeks Hall bequeathed this notable landmark to the National Trust for Historic Preservation and requested

Shadows-on-the-Teche

that the house be restored to the 30-year period of residence of his great grandmother, Mary Clara Conrad Weeks.

David Weeks, who died in 1834 before his new home was completed, left his widow Mary Clara and her six children to move into the Shadows alone. Undaunted, Mary Clara successfully managed the vast sugar plantations until her death during the Civil War. The personalities, interests, triumphs, and tragedies of Mary Clara and her family are very much a part of the interpretation of the Shadows, the furnishings of which realistically reflect their lifestyle.

The shadows of ancient oaks across the lawn gave the property its name. The beautifully preserved house contains the accumulated furniture, portraits, libraries, silver, and other treasures of four generations. The Shadows is one of the most well-documented houses in the area and has been named a National Historic Landmark by the Department of the Interior.

The significant architecture of The Shadows reflects the prevailing classical taste, with columns and architectural features of the Tuscan order. It is also a brilliant example of foreign influences that culminated in the distinctive style of the houses of the Louisiana countryside. The two-story home is constructed of rosy-colored brick, and is gracefully proportioned. It is situated among the lofty live oaks, and the attractive gardens contribute to its unique charm.

Open daily 9-4:30; nominal entrance fee. Closed Thanksgiving, Christmas, and New Year's Day.

Louisiana 14 off Highway 90, on Highway 182 West, 117 East Main Street, in New Iberia.

Justine

Justine

(OPEN TO PUBLIC)

Despite the fact that it is now 50 miles from its original site, this quaint cottage appears exactly as it did when it was built in 1822. The structure was shipped by barge on Bayou Teche from Centerville to its present site on La. 86, two miles east of New Iberia.

It is built entirely of native Louisiana cypress, and the honey-colored woodwork and Gothic stairway are unique. Furnished almost entirely in the Early Victorian style from the 1820s to 1850, its glassware, china, and furniture date from the 1700s to the present time. Early Louisiana pieces, both fine and primitive, have been recently added.

The Justine Bottle Museum on the grounds is believed to be the only such museum in the nation. Its shelves and counters hold an extensive collection of rare and unusual bottles.

Open 10:30-5; closed Monday and Tuesday except by appointment; call (318) 364-0973; nominal entrance fee.

On La. 86, two miles east of New Iberia.

Holleman House

The original house on this site was known as SEGURA HOUSE, constructed about 1812. Extended vacancy and two hurricanes damaged the house extensively, so a descendant of the Seguras had the house dismantled. Using materials and dimensions from the original, craftsmen completely rebuilt it. Private.

On Hwy. 182, west of New Iberia.

Dulcito

(OPEN BY APPOINTMENT)

Set in a grove of 300 oak, magnolia and pecan trees, this building dates back to 1788. It was built by Dauterive Dubuclet as a summer home, and is beautifully located on the banks of Spanish Lake (Lake Tasse).

During the War Between the States this home was used as a field hospital.

Its architectural style is typical of early Louisiana homes—a house raised on high pillars, with long gables and wide rambling galleries. The heavy cypress timbers of the frame and the exposed beams of the house are fastened with wooden pegs. Traces of the adobe walls of which the original structure was made may still be seen.

It was later purchased by the Trappey family and completely restored to its original beauty. The annual dinners of the Ancient Order of Creole Gourmets are held here.

Open by appointment only. Call (318) 369-3368. Seven miles west of New Iberia on Hwy. 182.

Dulcito

Duchamp

Built in the middle 1800's by Eugene Duchamp de-Chastagnier, an immigrant from Martinique, this plantation stands on top of a ridge. His town house, now the Post Office Building, in St. Martinville, is a replica of his sugar plantation home in the West Indies. Private.

On La. 96, four-and-a-half miles west of St. Martinville.

Acadian House Museum

(OPEN TO PUBLIC)

The house and the grounds on which it stands are all included in the Longfellow-Evangeline State Park, and were part of an original estate owned by D'Hauterive, who migrated here from France in 1763 or 1764.

61

Acadian House

The State of Louisiana purchased the house in 1931, and, after restoring it, opened it to the public in 1933. It had many smaller houses clustered around it — as was the rule with houses of this type — including a kitchen, smoke house, slave quarters, guest quarters and quarters for young, unmarried men of the family. The outbuildings connected were razed and have not been restored.

The great Evangeline Oak, believed to be over two hundred years old, is registered by the Live Oak Association. It is listed in the Hall of Famous Trees by the American Forestry Association because of its treasured historical significance.

Museum open Monday-Saturday, 9-5; Sunday, 1-5; closed Thanksgiving, Christmas, and New Year's Day; nominal entrance fee.

On La. 31, north of St. Martinville.

St. John

The large frame house is white with four tall wooden columns of classic style, a hipped roof and a belvedere. Leading through the grove in front of the house are an inner avenue of pines and an avenue of oaks. To the left of the grounds is a grove of orange trees.

It was built in 1828 by Alexandre Etienne de Clouet, descendant of the Chevalier Alexandre de Clouet, early commandant of the Poste de Attakapas.

A large wooded tract near the plantation was maintained as a deer park by de Clouet. Private.

On Hwy. 347, three miles north of St. Martinville.

Huron

This well-preserved plantation home was built prior to 1850 by Charles Lastrapes, a member of one of the old Creole families of the Attakapas country. It has a raised basement of dull red brick and a second floor of white-painted cypress. Private.

On La. 347, four-and-a-half miles south of Arnaudville.

Robin

Robin is a one-and-one-half-story cottage built by the son of one of Napoleon's generals. Private.

On the Bayou Teche River Road (La. 31), below Leonville.

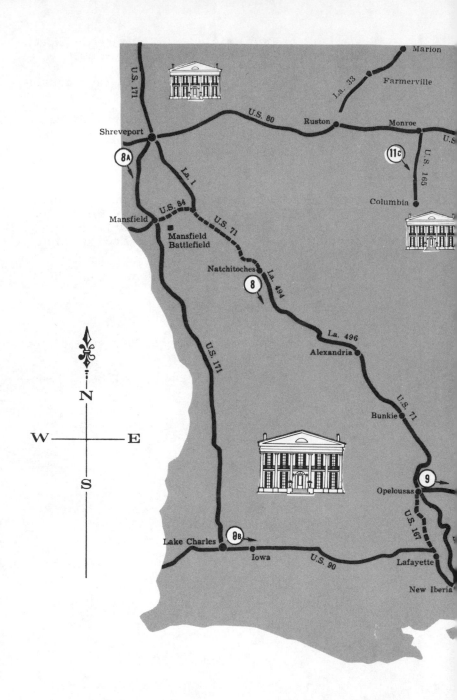

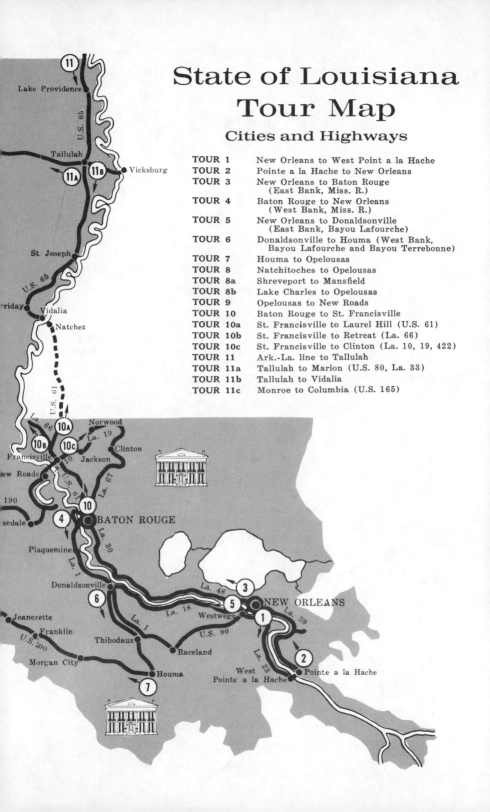

State of Louisiana
Tour Map
Cities and Highways

TOUR 8

Wells Home

(OPEN FOR GROUPS BY APPOINTMENT)

One of the oldest homes in Louisiana, this is the most authentically restored antebellum residence in Natchitoches. It was constructed around 1776 and features hand-hewn cypress sills and rafters joined with wooden pegs. The walls are adobe, mixed with dried moss and deer hair.

The residence once was known as the Williams-Tauzin home. Private.

At 607 Williams Avenue in East Natchitoches.

Lemee House

(OPEN TO PUBLIC BY APPOINTMENT)

Constructed by Trizzini and Soldini about 1830, this European style structure now serves as the headquarters for the Association for the Preservation of Historic Natchitoches. This was one of the few houses of the period with a cellar for smoked meats and wines. The one-and-one-half story plastered brick home, featuring a cradle roof, is a Natchitoches landmark.

The Lemee House serves as headquarters for the annual Fall Tour, sponsored by the Association for the Preservation of Historic Natchitoches, during the second weekend in October. Call (318) 352-2759 for appointments.

At 310 Jefferson Street.

Roque House

Constructed in the early 1800s, the ROQUE HOUSE is an excellent example of pioneer Louisiana construction. It is built with cypress beams and bousillage, walls filled with mud, animal hair, and moss. It is called the "Roque House" after its last occupant, Madame Aubin Roque, the granddaughter of Augustin Metoyer, a wealthy landowner in the Isle Brevelle section south of the city.

In 1967 Museum Contents, Inc., a non-profit organization, acquired the house and moved it to the present location on the river bank below Front Street. The structure is topped with an oversize roof of durable cypress shingles, forming a gallery around the house's exterior. Restoration was undertaken by the same organization.

The building now houses offices of Louisiana Outdoor Drama Association, producers of Paul Green's outdoor historical drama, "Louisiana Cavalier."

Open to the public Monday through Friday, 9-4. No admission charge.

Tante Huppe' House

The history and architecture of this old home are equally important, because it has played an important part in the lives of many area residents. The two-story structure was built for Suzette Prudhomme, Tante Huppé, in 1827. She was thrice married and her only son died in 1835. Until her death in 1861 Suzette lived alone, but her home served her many cousins, aunts, and other relatives when they were visiting in Natchitoches from neighboring plantations.

The house contains eighteen rooms. Walls are of cypress with brick between, typical of the early Louisiana architecture. The house plan has never been altered in any way. It has nine fireplaces and eleven outside doors. All of the locks, keys, curtain rods, and glass panes are original. The house was restored in 1968. Private.

424 Jefferson in Natchitoches.

Oaklawn Plantation

One of the distinguishing features of this beautiful antebellum house is the long avenue of live oak trees that line the front drive, believed to be the third longest avenue of oaks in Louisiana.

Oaklawn was built by Pierre Achille Prudhomme about 1840. The architecture is the raised Louisiana cottage, typical of the period, consisting of brick on the first level and wood on the second floor with adobe walls. The framework is hand-hewn cypress, pegged and mortised. The house remains for the most part in its original form. Private.

Open Tuesday-Sunday, 10-4.

Six miles south of Natchitoches on Hwy. 494.

Cherokee

CHEROKEE, dating back to the 1820s, is named for the Cherokee roses which adorn the front yard. The house is built in raised-cottage fashion, and is of cypress and bousillage construction. The six original fireplaces and tall folding doors of "faux bois" (false wood) add to the character of the house.

Now the property of Mr. and Mrs. William Nolan, Cherokee has been restored and refurnished with antiques from the Murphy family and with other early Louisiana style furniture. Mrs. Nolan is the granddaughter of the first Murphy to own the house. Private.

Cherokee is listed in the National Register of Historic Places.

On La. 494, about seven miles south of Natchitoches.

Beau Fort Plantation

(OPEN TO PUBLIC)

This wide cottage-type home, dating back to about 1830, was built for Narcisse Prudhomme I by his father. The current name was given to the home by its present owners, Mr. and Mrs. C. Vernon Cloutier, who completely restored the house and grounds in 1949. Mrs. Cloutier, at the time of her death in 1980, placed this wonderful gem of the past in care of the Association for the Preservation of Historic Natchitoches.

BEAUFORT contains many rare and interesting old pieces of furniture, and the garden boasts many beautiful rare flowers and trees.

Open daily, 1-4; groups invited; entrance fee.

On La. 119, about 10 miles south of Natchitoches.

Oakland

Oakland

Built in 1821 by slave labor, the plantation house is a large raised home with a 10-foot-deep veranda on all sides. Only the finest heart of cypress woods were used in its construction, joined entirely without nails. Walls of the supporting foundations are of brick and adobe, held together by deer hair and moss. The builder was Pierre Emmanuel Prudhomme, the third generation of his family in America and a successful planter of cotton, tobacco, and indigo. The eighth generation of the same family lives in the house today.

Among its many interesting furnishings are trundle and four-poster beds, oil paintings which were slashed by Union soldiers, handmade iron cooking utensils and tools, and curios. Drilling tools made by a slave blacksmith are also on display. The movie, "The Horse Soldiers," with John Wayne, was filmed here. Private.

La. 119, 10 miles south of Natchitoches.

Melrose

(OPEN TO PUBLIC)

Outstanding among the "Early Louisiana Type" plantations is Melrose Home Complex on the Cane River. The "Big House" is a raised cottage with the first floor of brick and the second of cypress. A rear wing and other improvements were later additions.

Melrose

At the left of the "Big House" is a cabin, formerly a slave hospital, built of cypress and chinked with mud and moss. To the rear is a square-shaped, hut-like structure of whitewashed brick, called the "African House." Its hipped, shingled roof was built with an extensive overhang to shelter wagons and teams. It has been named as one of the 13 distinctive buildings in the South by the federal government.

The plantation was established some time after 1750, and was originally called Yucca, after a Spanish dagger found nearby; the manor house was built in 1833 by Augustin Metoyer.

From 1875 until 1970 the plantation was the home of the Henry family, who changed its main crop from indigo to cotton, and renamed it after the Melrose Abbey, in Scotland.

MELROSE became a haven for writers and a center of the arts through the efforts of Mrs. Cammie Garret Henry. Among the many authors who enjoyed the hospitality of MELROSE over the years were Lyle Saxon, Alexander Woolcott, Francois Mignon, Rachel Field, Rose Franken, Gwen Bristow, Roark Bradford, and Harnett

African House at Melrose

Kane. Clementine Hunter, called "the black Grandma Moses" for her primitive paintings depicting plantation life, was once a cook here.

Now owned by the Association for the Preservation of Historic Natchitoches, MELROSE is listed by the National Register of Historic Places and has been designated a National Historic Landmark.

Open daily, 2-4:30; closed Monday and Wednesday. Entrance fee.

On Cane River, approximately sixteen miles south of Natchitoches, off Highway 1.

Bayou Folk Museum
(OPEN TO PUBLIC)

BAYOU FOLK MUSEUM, owned and operated by Northwestern State University, is housed in a typical early Louisiana home. Built between 1805 and 1813 by Alexis Cloutier for whom the town of Cloutierville is named, it was the home of author Katherine O'Flaherty Chopin (Kate Chopin) who made the Cane River and Natchitoches areas well known in her collection of creole short stories *Bayou Folk.*

The house, built by slave labor, is important because of its mortised peg construction, French doors, massive lower floor walls of bousillage, solid wood shutters, and outside stairways that provide the only entrance to the second floor. Bricks were used in the lower walls and front porch columns.

71

Bayou Folk Museum

The complex also includes a country doctor's office and a blacksmith shop, each containing interesting memorabilia of earlier days.

Listed in the National Register of Historic Places.

Open Saturday-Sunday, 1-5 (closed December, January and February, except the first weekend of December for the Natchitoches Christmas Festival). Open daily (June 1-August 15), Tuesday-Friday, 10-5, Saturday-Sunday, 1-5; other times by appointment. Entrance fee.

Off La. 1 on La. 495 in Cloutierville.

Magnolia

A one-and-one-half story house built a few years after the War Between the States, MAGNOLIA rests on the foundation of a former house burned during the war. Still standing at MAGNOLIA are the brick slave quarters, a row of tin-roofed houses built like tiny forts.

Ambrose Lecompte owned the plantation in the early nineteenth century. Mathew Hertzog, who built the present house, was the grandson of a former owner by the same name, who made MAGNOLIA the center of the southern racing world.

The house takes its name from a magnificent grove of magnolia trees, which, with the century-old oaks, forms one of the finest plantation home settings in the South. Private.

On La. 119, one mile north of Derry.

Chopin - Little Eva Plantation

(OPEN TO PUBLIC)

This location, formerly called "Hidden Hill," was known as CHOPIN PLANTATION after one of its owners, Lamy Chopin, Sr. Prior to the Chopin ownership, the plantation was owned by Robert McAlpin, a New Englander, and was called "The Old Robert McAlpin Plantation."

According to legend, McAlpin was the man after whom the character of Simon Legree was modeled, in the novel, **Uncle Tom's Cabin.** There has been a controversy over the years as to whether this was the original setting of the book, although one of the plantation's cabins was restored and exhibited as the "Original Uncle Tom's Cabin" in the Chicago World's Fair, in 1893.

The plantation is owned by Sterling Evans of Houston, Texas. The new owner renamed the plantation LITTLE EVA PLANTATION after the little heroine in the Harriet Beecher Stowe novel and has restored much of it to its original setting.

"Uncle Tom's Grave" and "Cabin" are open to the public; the main house is private.

Off La. 1, at Chopin, four miles south of Cloutierville. Continue south on La. 1.

Castille

Facing Bayou Rapides is CASTILLE, a raised cottage with a gabled roof. It was built some time prior to 1840. Private.

Off La. 496, seven miles from La. 1.

Eden Plantation House

This one-and-a-half-story frame house was built by Benjamin Kitchen Hunter before the War Between the States. Private.

On La. 496, seven-and-one-half miles from La. 1.

Tyrone

A beautiful old home which dates back to before the War Between the States, TYRONE has since been considerably remodeled. It was once the property of General Sprague, of New Orleans, and later of General Mason Graham. Private.

On La. 496, 15 miles from La. 1.

Cedar Grove

Notable for the thickness of its tongue-and-groove planking, CEDAR GROVE is believed to date from the middle 1700's — according to letters and papers found in an old chimney in the house. The style of the house is that of homes built in the early 1820's or 1830's, perhaps due to remodeling at that time.

CEDAR GROVE has outside staircases on its long front galleries, and white pillars in the classic design. It is now the home of Dr. and Mrs. Jack Cappel. Private.

On La. 496, about 15 miles from La. 1.

Kent House

(OUTBUILDINGS OPEN TO PUBLIC)

Kent House is believed to be the oldest standing structure in Central Louisiana and is a fine example of rural Louisiana architecture. The central section, built between 1796 and 1800 by Pierre Baillo, is of mud and moss—"bousillage" —between cypress beams. The two wings that flank the front gallery are later additions by the second owner, Robert Hynson, completed in the 1840s. Both the old and new portions of the house are raised high above the ground on brick piers. Inside are seven period rooms decorated with outstanding examples of Federal, Sheraton, and Empire furniture, as well as pieces made by native Louisiana cabinetmakers.

Four outbuildings are open to the public: a blacksmith shop, milk house, slave cabin, and carriage house. Plans have been made to move an old kitchen building to the property. In front of the main house is a formal parterre garden, while behind is an herb garden and a small orchard.

Open Monday through Saturday 9-5; Sunday 1-5. Closed

Kent House

Christmas, New Year's Day, and Thanksgiving. Nominal entrance fee.

On Bayou Rapides Road in Alexandria.

New Hope

This well-preserved two-story plantation house was built in 1816 by a member of the Tanner family. It has since been remodeled, but still retains the original frame house and foundation of heavy cypress timbers.

The house has wide porches which run the full length of the upper and lower floors, and slender wooden columns support the hipped roof. NEW HOPE faces Bayou Boeuf, and is set in a grove of pecan trees and an extensive flower garden. Private.

Off U. S. 71, two miles south of Meeker.

Loyd's Hall

(OPEN BY APPOINTMENT)

The uncertainty of the history of this mysterious two-and-one-half-story brick mansion enhances interest in it.

Loyd's Hall

75

Recent documentation provides information that this handsome house, whose owner wanted to have the showplace of the Boeuf, was built shortly before the Civil War. His neighbor, aging Civil War governor James Madison Wells, called the house "Loyd's Folly."

LOYD'S HALL features a double porch with white columns and iron lace trim. It faces north, overlooking Bayou Boeuf, near the old Lloyd Bridge which was used by travelers heading west along the "Texas Trail."

Legend has it that the house acquired its present spelling when a wayward member of the Lloyd family of England was given the property with the proviso that he leave Europe and change his name.

The house was restored by the late owner, Mrs. Virginia Fitzgerald, who refurnished the 20′ by 20′ by 16′ rooms. The original pine heart flooring, cypress woodwork and mahogany staircases are still in use. There is a dining table that dates back to 1743. Dr. Frank Fitzgerald and his wife now own the home. The antique shop on the grounds is open to the public.

Located near Meeker, off Highway 71.

Wytchwood

Built of hand-hewn cypress timbers held together with wooden pins, WYTCHWOOD stands at the end of a long avenue of moss-draped live oaks that leads in from the highway.

WYTCHWOOD is owned by the Robert Munson family, whose ancestors, Robert and Providence Tanner, settled the land around 1813. Private.

Off U. S. 71, one-and-one-half miles south of LOYD'S HALL.

Ewell Plantation House

Originally called CLARENDON, this house was built about 1850 for Martha Anne Koen as a wedding present from her father. It is a raised cottage, brick below and frame above, with a gabled, shingled roof. The original building constitutes the right half of the present structure. Private.

On La. 29, about five miles east of Bunkie.

Wright Plantation House

This mansion, surrounded by mammoth oak trees, is a two-story structure with a red brick foundation. The porch, with wooden Doric columns, encloses three sides. It was built in 1835 by Mr. S. M. Perkins, grandfather of the Wright family, after which family the house was later named.

According to family tradition, Sam Houston was lavishly entertained at this home on two occasions. Private.

On La. 29, about one mile past EWELL PLANTATION HOUSE. Return to Bunkie and U. S. 71; continue south to Lebeau, to junction with La. 10; turn right on La. 10 to Washington.

Homeplace

(OPEN TO PUBLIC)

Known for many years as "The Wikoff Place," HOME-PLACE is a story-and-one-half structure shadowed by a splendid grove of oaks. It was built in 1826 on a Spanish land grant of 1791 to Dr. Francois Robin, a native of France and a doctor of medicine and law.

The interior contains heirloom furnishings and rare furniture.

Open daily 10-4. For group tours, call (318) 826-7558; nominal entrance fee.

On Bayou Boeuf, five miles north of Washington, at Beggs.

Magnolia Ridge

(OPEN TO PUBLIC)

Completed in 1830, this superb mansion was originally known as the OLD PRESCOTT HOUSE and later as OAK-LAND PLANTATION. During the Civil War, it was head-quarters for both Confederate and Federal forces.

Built on a knoll overlooking Bayou Courtableau is this two-and-a-half-story brick house. It is of the conventional type of plantation house architecture, and is well over one hundred years old. It has six Doric plaster-covered brick columns which support the heavy cornice of the gabled roof.

Open by appointment only, daily 9-5. Call (318) 826-3967. Nominal entrance fee.

Six miles north of Opelousas on La. 10 and just off La. Highway 103, northwest of Washington.

Magnolia Ridge

Arlington

(OPEN TO PUBLIC)

Purchased, restored and occupied by Mr. and Mrs. Robert Olivier, it has been completely refurnished. Among its distinctive features are a wide central hallway of Italian flagstone on the lower level, a similar hallway reached by a mahogany-railed staircase on the second floor and a large school room on the third story.

Open daily 10-5; nominal entrance fee.

On Hwy. 103, two miles from Washington; turn right on lane for one-half mile.

Arlington

Wartelle House

This house is approached through one of the longest and most beautiful avenues of water oaks in Louisiana. Built in 1829 by Pierre Gabriel Wartelle — a captain in Napoleon's army who came to this area after Napoleon's exile to Elba — WARTELLE HOUSE is a one-story rambling white frame structure with a hipped dormer roof. Private.

Located west of Washington, about two hundred yards from Arlington.

Woodland

This well-preserved, interesting raised cottage was built in 1849. It is typical of construction of the period, with a main story of wood over a raised brick basement. The driveway leading to the house continues right through the basement to the rear of the house. Staircases lead to the gallery landing from each end of the basement driveway.

The roof, which projects over the gallery, is supported by six large round stuccoed-brick columns. Private.

East of Washington.

Means Plantation House

Constructed in a grove of lovely magnolia and oak trees, this late 18th century structure once served as the residence of an early French aristocrat, the Chevalier Florentin Poiret. It features round brick pillars in the lower gallery supporting smaller cypress columns of the upper gallery. The home has been completely restored by its present owners, the J. C. Means family. Private.

On La. 10 near Opelousas.

Ringrose Plantation House

Reported to be the oldest plantation home in St. Landry Parish, this beautiful two-story home with flanking quaint pigeonniers was built in 1770 by Michel Prudhomme, a member of the famous Natchitoches family.

A splendid example of early French plantation homes, RINGROSE is presently owned by Mrs. Austin Fontenot. Private.

At 1152 Prudhomme Circle in Opelousas.

Estorge Home

One of the older homes in the Opelousas area, this Greek Revival residence, featuring trompe l'oeil ceilings in the entrance hall and parlor, is a timeless landmark. It was constructed about 1830 by Pierre Labyche, who had it built with slave labor. Private.

At the corner of Market and Bloch streets in Opelousas.

Doucet House

A typical 18th century Louisiana French home, DOUCET HOUSE features cypress arched transoms over the ten French doors which came from the old St. Landry Courthouse.

The lower floor is constructed of brick, while the upper story is made of wood. One-story garconnieres are joined to each side of the house with covered galleries. Private.

Near Opelousas.

Linwood

Constructed in 1856 by Michel D. Boatwright and Caleb L. Swayze, Linwood was acquired by Dr. Vincent Boagni, grandfather of its present owner, in 1867.

Legend has it that the ghost of Capt. Jack Thompson, son-in-law of Dr. Boagni, frequently appears on the grounds. Antique shop open to the public.

Near Opelousas.

Charles Mouton House

This two-story home, once the center of a large plantation, was built in 1848 by Charles Mouton, who later served as Lieutenant Governor of Louisiana. The bottom floor is of white painted handmade brick, and the upper floor is of cypress.

Although restored and renovated many times, the main structure still retains its features. The live oaks still standing once were part of a large grove around the house. Private.

At 338 Sterling Avenue.

TOUR 8A

Land's End

(OPEN BY APPOINTMENT)

Now the home of the Henry F. Means family, this two-and-one-half-story frame house has fluted cypress columns of the Ionic order framing its gallery, and a gabled roof. It was built in 1857 by Mr. Means' great-grandfather, Col. Henry Marshall, of South Carolina, on a plantation which the colonel had established in 1835.

Land's End

The plantation received its name from Mrs. Marshall upon her arrival from South Carolina. As tradition tells it, when she learned that the Texas territory — then not part of the United States — was only about 20 miles to the west, she said her new home was "truly the end of the land."

LAND'S END played an important part in the Battle of Mansfield, in April, 1864. Many Confederate generals were frequent visitors to the home; and, after the battle, the house was used as a field hospital. The rugs and draperies were cut up and used as blankets for the wounded troops.

LAND'S END is now listed in the National Register of Historic Places.

Open to public by appointment; call (318) 925-0266; nominal entrance fee.

On Red Bluff Road, 17 miles south of Shreveport, via Linwood Road and Linwood Extension. Where extension ends, turn left on Red Bluff Road ¼ mile to the first private lane on the left. Drive up this road to home.

Buena Vista

This century-old home was built by Boykin Witherspoon, also of South Carolina. It is a three-story wooden house with octagonal wooden columns across the front. The gallery floor is detached from the columns which are set in square brick bases.

Within the home is an interesting square staircase, built when the house was erected from 1854-59.

In the fenced back yard stand the original cook house and a square, hand-hewn cypress log cabin that pre-dates the home.

Four miles south of Stonewall on Hwy. 171 to Red Bluff Road. Turn left, then drive one and one-half miles to the entrance. Private.

Roseneath

Built in the 1840's, ROSENEATH was the plantation home of the Means family — a name which has been part of the history of this section for more than 125 years; David B. Means and family, descendants of the original owner, now own and live in ROSENEATH.

The home is a two-story wooden structure with square wooden pillars on the upper and lower galleries, and has a galleried "ell" in the rear. At each end of the shingled, gabled roof is an outside chimney.

The house contains much of its original furniture which is still in use by the owners. Private.

Near Gloster.

Fairview

This raised cottage was constructed in 1848 on an original Spanish land grant. Complementing the splendid front gallery are French windows. Confederate soldiers camped here enroute to the Battle of Mansfield. There is a family cemetery near the road. Private.

On La. 172, about four miles past Keatchie.

Caspiana House

(OPEN TO PUBLIC)

CASPIANA HOUSE is part of the Pioneer Heritage Center in Shreveport. The house is of Georgian architecture, built in 1856, and was donated by the heirs of W. J. Hutchinson.

The complex also includes the detached kitchen from the Webb plantation, an 1860 double-pen log house and other structures. Visitors can glimpse how the early settlers in Northwest Louisiana lived and worked.

On the campus of Louisiana State University in Shreveport; open Sunday, 1:30-4:30 (except holidays). Group tours and school tours by appointment. Call (318) 797-5332.

TOUR 8B

Imperial Calcasieu Museum

(OPEN TO PUBLIC)

This lovely colonial building was constructed of beams from old homes in the area, bricks from the Missouri Pacific Railroad Station and columns from the old Majestic Hotel which once graced the city.

Now a museum, the building houses memorabilia from a century or more ago, including a 1607 "Breeches Bible," an old barber shop, ship's wheel, kitchen, and bedroom. In the rear of the new museum is the Sallier Oak, a 300-year-old tree named after the man after whom Lake Charles was named, Charles Sallier.

Open Monday-Friday, 10-12 and 2-5; Saturday, 10-12; Sunday, 2-5.

At 204 West Sallier Street.

LeBleu Plantation House

This one-story home, formerly two stories, with lower front gallery supported by six square cypress columns, includes within its walls materials of what is thought to have been the first dwelling ever built in this area by white men.

It is said that Lafitte and his pirate band frequently held meetings in the plantation's barn — which was destroyed in 1918. Another story about a later owner, "Grandma Joe" LeBleu, tells of how she fed two strangers who later turned out to be Jesse James and his brother, Frank. Private.

On U. S. 90, about five miles west of Iowa. Continue east to Lafayette.

Estherwood Manor

This stately two-story, Greek Revival home was purchased in 1976 by Gerald M. Martin and completely restored to its original beauty. The manor has eighteen rooms, five bedrooms on the second floor, five marble fireplaces, and large twin parlors which feature Gothic ceilings. Private.

On U. S. 90, 10 miles west of Crowley.

Blue Rose Museum

(OPEN BY APPOINTMENT)

More than 100 years old, this Acadian cottage was moved from Youngsville. Built of cypress, it has the original pegged construction, cypress paneling, handmade bricks, and mud and moss walls. Collections of fine china, cut glass, silver and antique furniture are on display. Rice cookbooks and other souvenirs are for sale.

Open weekdays by appointment. Closed holidays. Call (318) 783-3096.

Five miles southwest of Crowley.

Lafayette Museum

(OPEN TO PUBLIC)

The former home of Alexandre Mouton, Louisiana's first Democratic governor, this structure was built in 1800 by his father, Jean Mouton, as a large one-room house with a kitchen added at the back. Alexandre added three rooms to it and in 1849, when it was sold to Dr. W. G. Mills, the second and third floors and the lookout tower on the roof were added.

Open Tuesday through Saturday, 9-12 and 2-5; Sunday, 3-5. Closed Monday and holidays.

At 1122 Lafayette Street.

Shady Oaks

This house was built in 1848 for Charles Homere Mouton, grandson of Jean Mouton, one of the first settlers in Lafayette Parish. The lower floor is handmade brick and the upper floor is cypress wood.

It is an interesting blend of French and Anglo-American design. Restored many times, it still retains its original charm and architectural features.

The live oaks still standing were once part of a large grove around the house. Private.

Located at 338 North Sterling St. in Lafayette.

Myrtle Plantation House

Built in 1811 by Dr. Matthew Creighton, the first physician to practice in the city of Lafayette, this antebellum home has been added to by each succeeding generation. Creighton is famous for having failed the first medical licensure test ever given in Louisiana. He sued, and in court was able to recall all the questions of the test and give the answers from memory! In spite of this remarkable feat, he lost his suit, but passed the next examination. The present hall of the house, with its hand-hewn stairway at the rear, was originally the front porch of the old house and was closed in with shutters and transoms.

On the canvas walls and ceiling of the present dining room are landscaped scenes painted about 70 years ago by Charles de Bubuire, a French artist who had worked on the old French Opera House in New Orleans. Private.

Hugh Wallis Road, near Lafayette.

Chretien Point

(OPEN TO PUBLIC)

This two-story blood-red brick home was built in 1831 by Hypolite Chretien II on land which was a wedding gift from his father, Hypolite I.

Originally granted to Pierre Declouet by the Spanish government in 1776, the land came under Chretien ownership at the close of the 18th century.

The mansion is built on a slight rise which adds to its massive stateliness. It has six white columns set in square bases rising past the upper gallery to the hipped roof. Three large doors, each separated by a window, open on the first- and second-floor galleries. Both the doors and windows are curved at the top in well-rounded arches.

Lafitte the pirate was a close friend of the elder Chretien and a frequent visitor to the plantation.

Approximately three miles southwest of Sunset; drive west on La. 182, south on La. 754 for 200 yards, left on parish road for about two miles.

TOUR 9

Woodley Plantation House

This one-and-one-half-story frame house, well over a century old, is located on the Woodley Plantation. The plantation was established by Isaac Johnson, Governor of Louisiana from 1846 to 1850, after he moved to this area from West Feliciana Parish. Private.

On La. 411, one mile south of Livonia. Continue south of Maringouin, on La. 77.

Sunnyside

Built prior to 1855, SUNNYSIDE was first owned by Capt. Jesse Hart. The house is a raised cottage type, with a cypress upper story over a plastered-brick basement. Private.

Off La. 77, in the Maringouin vicinity.

El Dorado

Once owned by the famous Barrow family, of the Felicianas, EL DORADO is a beautiful, white dormered cottage which dates back to the early 1800's.

Of special interest is the two-story brick slave quarters, located directly behind the main house. Private.

Off La. 77, in the Maringouin vicinity.

Tanglewild

Built within a grove of giant live oaks, TANGLEWILD is a one-story white frame building constructed by Bartholomew Barrow prior to the War Between the States. There are several interesting and old family portraits within the house. Private.

Just off La. 77, directly across from the Bayou Grosse Tete Bridge, in the Maringouin vicinity.

Mound Plantation House

Constructed by Austin Woolfolk well over a century ago, MOUND PLANTATION HOUSE was named after the Indian mound on which it was built. It is a rambling single-story frame cottage, with an ell on one side. In the rear is a slave laundry made of brick.

During the construction, a number of Indian relics were uncovered, including human skeletons. Private.

On La. 77, three miles south of Maringouin.

Shady Grove Plantation House

One of the many plantations owned by Capt. Joseph Erwin, SHADY GROVE was purchased from him by his son in 1828. The house, built in 1858, is a two-story brick structure with wooden Ionic columns on the lower floor, and Corinthian columns on the upper.

The building is now used as a school. Private.

On La. 77, about four miles south of Maringouin.

Live Oaks Plantation House

The house and plantation were established by Charles Dickinson, of Tennessee, who was the grandson of Capt. Joseph Erwin. Dickinson's father was killed in a duel with Andrew Jackson.

LIVE OAKS HOUSE is a white, green-shuttered frame building of two-and-one-half stories. It has galleries across the front which are supported by six square wooden pillars, and is set in a grove of superb live oaks — one of which is almost 30 feet in circumference. Within the grove is a slave church, built of red brick and set off with faded green blinds. Private.

On La. 77, just north of Rosedale.

Trinity Plantation House

This one-and-one-half-story house was built by Dr. George Campbell, of New Orleans, in 1839. It is a plaster-covered brick structure which stands on an Indian mound at the end of a splendid avenue of live oaks.

The house was beautifully restored by a later owner. Private.

On La. 77, southern end of Rosedale. Return to U. S. 190; turn east about seven miles to junction with La. 1; turn north on La. 1 to False River and New Roads.

Austerlitz

A typical two-story frame house with a brick basement, Austerlitz is encircled by a gallery 80 feet wide and 14 feet deep. The second floor is of cypress, reinforced with brick and mortar. It has square wooden pillars below and slender columns above, and both upper and lower entrances are fan-lighted.

AUSTERLITZ was built in 1832 on land purchased from two Indian chiefs by Joseph Decuir, 35 years earlier. An architect was brought in from Santo Domingo to design the house, which accounts for its decided West Indies influence.

In 1899, a two-story annex was added, increasing the number of rooms to 22.

The house was named for one of Napoleon Bonaparte's battles.

Locke Breaux, brother of Chief Justice Joseph Breaux of the Louisiana Supreme Court, was a late owner. Private.

On La. 1, six miles south of New Roads, along False River.

Parlange

Parlange

(OPEN TO PUBLIC)

Built in 1750 by the Marquis Vincent de Ternant on False River, PARLANGE is one of Louisiana's oldest and most charming plantation homes. It is of the "Early Louisiana Type," designed for comfort and fashioned out of materials on hand.

Its two stories are a raised brick basement and a second floor of cypress, with twin chimneys atop the roof. Galleries completely encircle the house and twin brick pigeonniers are at either side. All are painted white and trimmed in green.

Originally an indigo plantation, PARLANGE was changed to a sugar cane plantation in the 19th century by Claude Vincent de Ternant, son of the builder.

Designated a historic building by Secretary of the Interior Harold A. Ickes, PARLANGE typifies the tastes and tradition of the antebellum period.

In 1970 PARLANGE also was designated a National Historic Landmark.

PARLANGE was occupied by both Gen. Nathaniel Banks of the Union Army and Gen. Dick Taylor of the Confederacy at different times during the Red River Campaign in 1864.

Still a working plantation, the home has been occupied by descendants of the original builder since 1750. Three generations of Parlanges reside here today.

The two dovecotes, on each side of the front drive, are constructed of handmade brick and are, perhaps, the only octagonal ones in America.

On La. 1, five miles south of New Roads.

Desfosse' House

(OPEN TO PUBLIC)

Early records and exhaustive research indicate that the original house was built about 1790. In 1850 Dr. Jules Charles Desfossé purchased the "land and improvements" and began extensive renovations to change the appearance to suit his more Anglo-Saxon taste. The house today is a fine example of a mid-nineteenth century planter's house. A native of Orleans, France, Dr. Desfossé, whose ancestors were chemists, became a prominent doctor in the Mansura area.

The one-and-a-half-story house reflects the typical construction of the period—"bousillage entre poteaux," dried mud between posts. The exterior walls are covered with beaded boarding.

Restoration of this historic home was directed by La Commission Des Avoyelles and other organizations and individuals. The home is open to the public during scheduled hours.

In Mansura; La. 1, 50 miles northwest of New Roads.

Defosse House

TOUR 10

Linwood

Built by Gen. Albert G. Carter in 1838-40, this large white two-story plantation home remained in the Carter family until 1910.

It has four brick Doric columns across the front, and galleries on both the lower and upper floors.

During the War Between the States, Union troops used LINWOOD as a hospital. Private.

Left, one mile off U. S. 61, 12 miles north of Baton Rouge.

Oakley

Oakley Plantation
Audubon State Park

(OPEN TO PUBLIC)

OAKLEY is famed as the plantation where John James Audubon first became acquainted with the wildlife of the Feliciana Country. No place in Louisiana is richer in memories of the naturalist. It is now the site of the Audubon Memorial State Park, a 100-acre tract set aside as a wildlife sanctuary, and provides overnight trailer and picnic facilities.

The plantation was built from 1795-99 by Ruffin Gray. His widow married James Pirrie. Their daughter, Eliza Pirrie, "belle of the Felicianas," was a pupil of Audubon.

It is a two-story frame house built over a raised brick basement. A curved stairway joins the two galleries, and the house has a simple, air-swept appearance that fits its location.

Minimal admission to park. Scheduled tours of OAKLEY HOUSE MUSEUM free.

Open Monday-Saturday, 9-4:45; Sunday, 1-4:45. Children under 12 free. Closed Christmas, Thanksgiving and New Year's Day.

On Highway 965, east of St. Francisville.

Oakley Garden

93

The Browse

This home was constructed on a section of Troy Plantation, an original Spanish land grant to Isaac Johnson, a partner of John Mills, the founder of St. Francisville. The house is particularly noted for its lovely garden and historic memorabilia. Private.

On La. 965, east of St. Francisville.

TOUR 10A

Propinquity

PROPINQUITY is a townhouse constructed in 1809 by the widow of John H. Mills, who founded St. Francisville and Bayou Sara.

Used as a store in 1822, the structure faithfully reflects the Spanish Colonial period in the history of the Felicianas. Private.

Overnight accommodations with continental breakfast available.

Listed in the National Register of Historic Places.

523 Royal Street in St. Francisville.

Virginia

The oldest house in historic St. Francisville, VIRGINIA dates from 1790 when its original structure was used as a store.

Purchased in 1817 by a Philadelphia merchant, it was then used to house a business. Additions to the house were built in 1829 and 1856 when the Victorian two-story wing was constructed. Private.

On Royal Street in St. Francisville.

Camilla Leake Barrow Home

The oldest house used continuously as a private residence in St. Francisville, the CAMILLIA LEAKE BARROW HOME has been in the Leake family since 1866.

The house's two-story section was built between 1810 and 1817 by Amos Webb. The cottage was added about 1858 by J. Hunter Collins as a law office. Private.

At the corner of Johnson and Royal streets in St. Francisville.

The Myrtles

(OPEN TO PUBLIC)

This is a one-and-a-half story house with wide, 110-foot-long verandas, and ornamented with elaborate iron grillwork. It is set in a live oak grove which is a blaze of color in the spring.

Built about 1830, the home is in an excellent state of preservation — especially the interior, which is highlighted

The Myrtles

by intricate plaster moldings in each room, the glass-coated original silver door knobs and the remarkable condition of the colonial wallpaper in the entry hall. The home, including interior, was presented on CBS-TV in 1971.

Another interesting feature of THE MYRTLES is that it is popularly reputed to have at least one "ghost."

Open daily; nominal entrance fee.

On U.S. 61 at St. Francisville.

Catalpa

(OPEN TO PUBLIC)

This Victorian-type cottage was built in 1885 on one of the oldest antebellum home sites in Louisiana and is still in the family of the original owners.

Noteworthy features include its beautiful antique furniture and a double-horseshoe alley of live oaks hung with Spanish moss lining the drive. A 30-acre garden shows almost every variety of plant and tree native to the state.

Open daily, 9-5; closed December and January, except by appointment. Nominal entrance fee.

On La. 61, five miles north of St. Francisville.

Catalpa

Rosale

This plantation was originally called EGYPT when it was established by Alexander Stirling on a Spanish land grant in 1790. It was also known as CHINA LODGE when David Barrow purchased it in 1844, five years before he built AFTON VILLA. ROSALE was given its present name by Robert Hilliard Barrow — son-in-law of David — when he received it as a wedding gift.

In 1810, this plantation was the site of the first public mass meeting when the Feliciana planters gathered here to free the land of Spanish rule. Private.

Off U. S. 61, about seven miles north of St. Francisville.

Wakefield Plantation House

Established in 1833 by Lewis Stirling — son of Alexander Stirling — WAKEFIELD PLANTATION HOUSE was a two-and-a-half-story columned structure of imposing proportions. It was named after Goldsmith's novel, **The Vicar of Wakefield.**

Lewis Stirling was one of the outstanding figures in the West Florida parishes rebellion against Spain, and it was he who urged the planters to hold the first public mass meeting at EGYPT (ROSALE), which later blossomed into open revolt, and then independence.

Stirling willed the property to his heirs, to be divided into three parts. Two heirs retained the first floor section — now occupying the present site; the upper floor and attic were physically removed in 1878 and constructed into cottages. Both have since burned.

Open 9-4 daily, Sunday 1-4; entrance fee; overnight accommodations with continental breakfast available.

On U. S. 61, about eight miles north of St. Francisville.

The Cottage

(OPEN TO PUBLIC)

This low, rambling two-story house with an exceptionally long front gallery is, in reality, a series of buildings erected from 1795 to 1859 around an original structure in the Spanish tradition. It was built completely of virgin cypress, except for its massive 16' by 16' sills of blue poplar wood. Twelve posts support the gabled roof.

This, the ancestral home of the Butler family, was bought in 1811 by Judge Thomas Butler, who practiced law in the Florida parishes.

THE COTTAGE is surrounded by many of the original plantation outbuildings, including slave quarters.

Gen. Andrew Jackson was a visitor here, in 1815, en route to Natchez after his victory at New Orleans. Tradition states that he and his large group of officers, including his chief of staff, Gen. Robert Butler, brother of the host, and seven other Butlers, so inconvenienced the host that he had to sleep in the pantry.

"The Fighting Butlers" loom large in American history. Col. Thomas Butler (father of the judge) was one of five brothers in the Revolutionary army commended for gallantry by Washington, Lafayette and Wayne. Another of the five, Maj. Gen. Richard B. Butler, placed the American flag on the British works at Yorktown after Cornwallis surrendered. Capt. Richard Butler, a cousin of the judge, became owner of ORMOND PLANTATION in 1802.

THE COTTAGE boasts a number of historic treasures and letters concerning the great figures of early America. Still in possession of descendants is the original land grant signed by the Baron de Carondelet, in 1795.

There are mementoes used at a banquet given by Dr. Newton Mercer, of New Orleans, for the Grand Duke Alexis of Russia, in 1872. Open to the public; nominal fee charged. Mr. and Mrs. J. E. Brown are the present owners.

Open daily 9-5 except Christmas Day. Overnight guests are served plantation breakfasts. Call (504) 635-3674 for reservations.

On U. S. 61, nine miles north of St. Francisville.

The Cottage

Laurel Hill

Built on a 216-acre Spanish land grant in the 1820's, LAUREL HILL was the home of the Argue family. It is constructed of hand-hewn logs, covered with clapboard. The lower gallery has six square wooden columns; the upper gallery is smaller and partly enclosed.

Just beyond LAUREL HILL HOUSE is St. John Episcopal Church, erected in 1873. Private.

On U. S. 61, at Laurel Hill.

TOUR 10B

Highland Plantation House

This lovely two-story home of cypress, blue poplar and hand-burned brick was built in 1804 by William Barrow on a 3,600-acre Spanish land grant.

The house, with the exception of the window blinds, was constructed solely of materials built, finished or hand-wrought on the plantation by slave labor. The blinds were made in Cincinnati, Ohio, from cypress logs cut on the plantation.

Originally called LOCUST RIDGE, the plantation was renamed HIGHLAND to honor a new variety of cotton grown there by William's son, Bennet—who also planted 150 live oaks around the house in 1832.

HIGHLAND contains superior cabinet-work and hand-carved wainscoting, door and window frames, and its most unusual feature is a Palladium window on the upper floor. It is now owned by the Barrow Norwood family, direct descendants of the Barrows.

Open by appointment only. For further information contact the West Feliciana Historical Society, P. O. Box 338, St. Francisville, La. 70775, (504) 635-6330.

Off La. 66, five miles north of Bains.

Feliciana

This beautiful home was built in 1830. It has a fanlighted doorway and six large white columns in front. It is considered one of the loveliest antebellum homes in the area. Private.

Off La. 66, six miles north of Bains (near the site of the now-burned Greenwood Plantation House).

Ellerslie

A tall, square, white plastered-brick structure, the home is surrounded by wide upper and lower galleries. Doric columns rise from the lower-floor gallery up to the hipped roof.

ELLERSLIE was built in 1835 by Judge William C. Wade, a millionaire from the Carolinas. It was later occupied by the Percy family, whose daughters were pupils of John James Audubon.

Originally a cotton and cane plantation, it is now a cattle ranch, and still owned by descendants of the original Percy family. ELLERSLIE is ranked as one of the two most perfect examples of Greek Revival construction in the Deep South, and as the classical Louisiana Plantation Home. Private.

One mile off La. 66, on Bayou Sara, eight miles north of Bains.

Rosebank Plantation House

Constructed of cypress over a high brick basement, this house is said to be an old Spanish inn established in 1790 by John O'Connor who served as **alcalde** (Sp. magistrate) of the district.

The house has long galleries across the front, which are supported by round brick Doric columns. While extensive alterations have been made on the house, it is almost the same as it looked when first erected. It was later owned by the Barrow family. Private.

Off La. 66, seven-and-a-half miles north of Bains.

Live Oak Plantation House

Said to have been built about 1802, LIVE OAK PLANTATION HOUSE is a two-story brick building set flush on the ground. It has four squat stucco-covered brick pillars supporting the second-floor gallery, and was once owned by a member of the Barrow family.

Built by Cyrus Ratliff, the home has recently been completely restored. Open by appointment only.

On La. 66, eight-and-a-half miles north of Bains.

Weyanoke

A two-story frame house with gabled roof and plastered front, WEYANOKE housed a school where the wife of John James Audubon taught in the 1820s.

Originally a log-cabin, the house had an upper story added in 1856 by Major John Towles. Audubon certainly was a frequent visitor and may have used a subject from the plantation for his "Wild Turkey" painting. Private.

Just off La. 66, 15 miles northwest of St. Francisville.

Retreat Plantation House

Established in the early 1850s by Capt. Clarence Mulford, this plantation was originally called SOLDIER'S RETREAT. It is situated on a bluff overlooking Little Bayou Sara, and stands in a grove of moss-hung live oak trees. The dormered roof is supported by four round stuccoed-brick columns. Private.

On La. 66, at Retreat (11 miles north of Bains). Return to junction with La. 10, at St. Francisville. Continue east on La. 10 (Tour 10c) to BELMONT.

TOUR 10C

Locust Grove Site

This site was once the plantation home of the Luther L. Smiths, and it was established on a Spanish grant prior to 1816. Mrs. Smith—the former Anna Eliza Davis—was the sister of Jefferson Davis, president of the Confederacy.

The plantation was destroyed by fire, and only the scattered bricks of a small game house remain.

Center of interest in the grounds is a little shaded cemetery in which the Smiths are buried. Also buried there is Sarah Knox Taylor Davis—who, tradition says, became the first wife of Jefferson Davis by eloping with him, after failing to get permission to marry from her father, later President Zachary Taylor. She died in 1835.

Another grave is that of Gen. Eleazer W. Ripley, hero of the Battle of Lundy's Lane, near Niagara Falls, in the War of 1812.

Off La. 10, east of St. Francisville.

Wildwood

WILDWOOD, once the summer home of the Soule family of New Orleans, is a nine-bedroom, three-story mansion dating from 1915 and has been completely restored.

Situated on a 450-acre plantation near Rosedown, the home lay in disrepair for many years until 1958 when it was fully restored.

The structure contains many family heirlooms and other treasures, including a signed Mallard sideboard, an antique playpen, a pedal-operated washing machine and a hand-carved rosewood set, a wedding gift to the original owners, the Albert Soules. Private.

Located off Highway 10, northeast of St. Francisville, near Rosedown.

Rosedown

(OPEN TO PUBLIC)

A two-story house with wings of cement-covered brick, its six columns support wide front verandas. Its formal garden were copied after those at Versailles by the French landscape gardener who designed the original. Marble statues of the gods and goddesses of mythology and Italian statuary abound. The house represents a blending of the Louisiana, Georgian and classic styles.

It was built in 1835 by Daniel Turnbull — a descendent of George Washington — for his wife Martha Hilliard Barrow Turnbull, who named it ROSEDOWN.

The land of ROSEDOWN PLANTATION was a Spanish land grant to John Mills in 1789, one of the founders of St. Francisville.

A magnificent restoration has made ROSEDOWN Plantation and Gardens one of America's most distinguished showplaces.

Open March-November, 9-5; December-February, 10-4. Entrance fee.

On La. 10, about two miles east of St. Francisville.

Rosedown

Roseneath

Roseneath

(OPEN BY APPOINTMENT)

Now the home of Mrs. A. P. Acosta and Mr. and Mrs. Henry Johnston, ROSENEATH dates back to 1830. At one time it served as a school for the children of Jackson.

This two-story building features fluted Doric columns and a graceful winding stairway. The house contains lovely antiques, a Nancy glass collection, relics from the War Between the States and a century-old scrapbook.

In Jackson. Continue east on La. 10 to junction of La. 68. South on La. 68 to ASPHODEL.

Milbank

(OPEN TO PUBLIC)

This classic Greek structure was built in the mid-1830s. A two-story home with double galleries, it has served as a hotel, bank, and private home. It is furnished with fine antiques from nearby Centenaria (1840).

Open by appointment. Group tours. Call (504) 634-7273 or (504) 634-7155. Entrance fee.

On Bank Street, one block off La. 10 in Jackson.

Asphodel

(OPEN TO PUBLIC)

An example of the Greek Revival style, ASPHODEL was built about 1833 by Benjamin Kendrick, whose daughter was a pupil of Audubon.

It consists of a raised central structure and two identical wings of brick, covered with a smooth plaster which was made by slaves using sand from a nearby creek. A wide gallery crosses the front of the main building, and six white Doric columns support the gabled roof which has two dormer windows. Each wing is a miniature of the central building, and each has a small porch.

It has been charmingly restored and is now the home of Mr. and Mrs. Robert E. Couhig. ASPHODEL was used during the filming of "The Long Hot Summer," which starred Joanne Woodward, Paul Newman and Orson Wells.

ASPHODEL Mansion itself is open by appointment 10-4, Monday-Friday; closed Saturday, Sunday and holidays.

Asphodel

Inn, guest house and gift shop are housed in separate buildings. Meals served at Inn every day except Christmas. Call (504) 654-5820 for reservations. Nominal entrance fee to mansion.

Twenty-five miles north of Baton Rouge, on La. 68.

Lakeview

Built in the 1840's by William East, LAKEVIEW has been beautifully restored by its present owners, Dr. and Mrs. Kernan Irwin, and is their country estate.

The house is a two-storied, white frame structure and has a front gallery crossing its entire length. Of particular interest is the old brick kitchen, which is still in its original condition.

The furnishings are antique, in keeping with the era of its construction. Private.

On La. 963, between Gurley and Clinton. Return to junction with La. 19; proceed north on La. 19 to Wilson.

Glencoe Plantation

(OPEN TO PUBLIC)

This beautiful frame home has been called the finest example of Queen Anne Victorian architecture in the state.

It was first built in 1870. After it was completely destroyed by fire, the owner, Emmerson Thompson, rebuilt the structure to the exact specifications.

Will Rogers, Sr. and Tom Mix were frequent visitors on cattle buying trips to Thompson Plantation.

Listed in the National Register of Historic Places.

Open Monday-Saturday, 10-4; Sunday, 1-4. Entrance fee. Overnight accommodations with breakfast available, call (504) 629-5387.

On La. 68, south of Wilson.

Oakland

Built in 1827 by Judge Thomas W. Scott of South Carolina, this home shows obvious architectural influences of his native state.. Raised on brick pillars interspaced with lattice, the house has a wide front gallery running its entire length. Above the gallery's slanting roof is a line of shutters. The eaves are high and the roof is steep. Two large double doors, almost eight feet across, highlight the front entrance.

Features of the house include woodwork of the Federal Period, beaded boards for walls, plank ceilings and unusual mantels. A spacious corridor runs through the house. Private.

Eight miles west of Clinton, near Gurley.

The Shades

This two-story red brick home was built by Alexander Scott about 1808 on land which was granted to him. Bordering the brick walk leading to the entrance is tall boxwood, and ivy twines its way around the thick white porch columns.

The kitchen, a main wing of the home, is built flush with the ground and has cemented porches enclosed by narrow columns.

The late Miss Eva Scott, great-granddaughter of the original builder, lived at THE SHADES until her death. Miss Scott was widely known for her interesting collection of almost 1,000 old bells.

On La. 952, about three miles west of Wilson. Continue on La. 952 to HICKORY HILL.

Hickory Hill

Built about 1810 by David McCants, of South Carolina, HICKORY HILL is a tall narrow building of red brick. On the front are four white plastered-brick columns which rise to the fanlighted pediment. The columns are of the Doric order; the outer two are square and the inner two round.

Both the upper and lower galleries are enclosed at each end by a brick wall.

During the War Between the States, the 15-year-old son of the family who was home on furlough was forced to hide in a childhood hiding-place under the attic steps to avoid being captured by Union troops who searched the house. Private.

On La. 952, about one mile past THE SHADES. Return to Wilson, to junction with La. 19; north on La. 19 to Norwood. Junction with La. 422, east to RICHLAND.

Richland

This is one of the most palatial homes in the Felicianas. It was built by Elias Norwood in 1820 for his bride, Katherine Chandler, of South Carolina.

Construction is of white painted brick with four Doric columns in the front portico. The brick was made from native clay by slave labor. Inside, however, a fine contrasting elegance is found. An exquisite unsupported spiral stairway soars to the third floor, and beautiful Italian marble mantels adorn each room on the lower floor. Private.

On La. 422, five miles east of Norwood.

Richland

Bonnie Burn

Now the home of Mr. and Mrs. Richard Kilbourne, BONNIE BURN was built prior to 1847 by James Holmes. It was purchased in 1868 by J. G. Kilbourne, a Clinton lawyer, Confederate Army captain and great-grandfather of the present owner.

BONNIE BURN (Scottish for Pretty Creek which flows nearby) was fired upon by Federal troops, and fragments of a Confederate cannon may be seen. The house has beautiful furnishings which are typical of its period of construction. Private.

In Clinton, northwest section.

Bennett-Brame House
(OPEN BY APPOINTMENT)

Built in 1840, this house is an example of Greek Revival architecture. Six Doric columns in front support the pediment which contains a unique sliding fan shaped window.

The delicacy of the ornamentation above the doorways and windows is of particular interest, as is the graceful winding stairway in the hall.

The restored slave quarters and kitchen are to the back of the house, as is the circular-shaped well shed, which is also of the Greek Revival style of architecture.

Owned by the Brame-Bennett families for five generations, the home is presently owned by Mrs. William Thomas Bennett. It is the only residence in East Feliciana Parish chosen for a permanent graphic record in the Library of Congress by the Historic Buildings Survey. The home is listed in the National Register of Historic Places. Private. (Open by appointment only; call (504) 683-5241; nominal entrance fee.)

Overnight accommodations and breakfast available.

In Clinton on La. 67.

110

Lane Plantation Home

Constructed about 1825 by the Weston family, LANE PLANTATION HOME reflects the distinctive South Carolina architectural influence. Of clapboard construction atop brick pillars, the home also includes country English influences.

Purchased by William Allen Lane in 1830. the home is now owned by his descendants, the A. Lane Plauche family, and stands exactly as it did originally, except for the addition of a kitchen wing on the west and a master bedroom wing on the east. The doors and interior walls are of plank. Six dining chairs and a child's high chair, all crafted on the plantation, are among the home's original pieces. Original panes of glass remain in many of the windows.

Family mementoes to be found on display include the peg leg of James Tyson Lane, which he wore after losing a leg in the Civil War, an old ruffle iron, a brass bullet mold, some old christening dresses and several old Bibles.

Restoration by the present owners was completed in 1969. Private.

Off La. 955, eight miles southwest of Clinton.

Avondale Plantation

(OPEN TO PUBLIC)

Built around 1830 by David and Elizabeth d'Armond, this Greek Revival raised cottage was moved to its present location in 1981 and restored to its original beauty. The furnishings include many Early American primitive and country pieces.

Listed in the National Register of Historic Places.

Open Monday-Saturday, 10-5; Sunday, 1-5; entrance fee. Overnight accommodations and breakfast available; call (504) 683-5004 or (504) 387-4330.

Off La. 10, east of Clinton.

Stonehenge

Built on a hill among large oak trees, which enhance the beauty of many early pioneer homes of the area, STONEHENGE dates from 1837.

Judge Lafayette Saunders built this imposing Greek Revival home, as well as the magnificent East Feliciana Courthouse and a law office on Lawyer's Row.

A unique feature of the interior of the home is a wooden lattice screen that divides the front and back hall and is thought to be the only one of its kind in the country. Private.

On La. 67, south, in Clinton.

Plovanich Place

(OPEN BY APPOINTMENT)

PLOVANICH PLACE is another wonderful example of the restoration in the Clinton area.

The lovely home was rebuilt from the Hunter Brothers Store (circa 1870) of Waterproof, Louisiana, with the original red cypress wood and unusual wood siding simulating stone.

It is said that Huey P. Long made his first political speech from the front gallery.

Open by appointment, entrance fee. Overnight accommodations and breakfast available. Call (504) 683-8927.

On La. 63, south of Clinton (off La. 67).

Marston House

(OPEN TO PUBLIC)

Originally built as a bank in 1838, MARSTON HOUSE is now the headquarters for the East Feliciana Pilgrimage and Garden Club.

This stately building was placed in the National Register of Historic Places in 1971, and is now in the process of being restored. It serves as Hostess House for guests and visitors who tour the area. Open Tuesday and Friday, 10-4; Sunday, 2-5; entrance fee. Call (504) 683-8927 or (504) 683-8708.

In Clinton, southeast section, Bank Street, continue south on La. 67.

Blairstown

This two-story home, built in 1850 by Samuel Lee, is a fine example of the Greek Revival style of architecture. It was constructed by slave labor who cut the timber and made the brick on the property. Horse hair was mixed in with the plaster to bind it more efficiently, and square-shaped nails were used in the construction.

Now the home of Mr. and Mrs. Bob R. Jones, whose children are the fifth generation of the family to live there, BLAIRSTOWN has four-poster Louisiana beds and an old sugar chest; also of interest is the old family cemetery nearby. Private.

On La. 959, at Blairstown, five miles west of La. 67. (See Tours 4 and 9.)

Martin Hill

(OPEN TO PUBLIC)

Named for the many purple martins who inhabited the grounds of a former owner, MARTIN HILL is a lovely Greek Revival raised cottage and dates back to around 1840.

Heinrich Mayer, a prominent merchant in Clinton, enlarged the home around 1900. The elaborate front doors still show the initial "M" in glass. Among other remarkable features of this home are the interior doors and staircase.

Open by appointment, entrance fee. Call (504) 683-8281 or (504) 683-5594.

On St. Helena St. E. (La. 10) in Clinton.

Irwin House

(OPEN TO PUBLIC)

This imposing Colonial Revival mansion, circa 1903, has been restored and houses a group of shops, a restaurant and lounge.

Open Monday-Saturday, 10-4.

On St. Helena St. (La. 10) and Plank Road (La. 67) in Clinton.

Old Wall Parsonage

(OPEN BY APPOINTMENT)

The Reverend Isaac Wall, a Methodist circuit rider, and his wife, Mary Winans, daughter of a prominent Methodist clergyman, built the original parsonage in 1840.

Open by appointment, entrance fee. Call (504) 683-8402 or (504) 346-0813.

On Woodville St. in Clinton.

TOUR 11

Ashtabula

This prominent home was built about 1845 in the typical architectural style of the period. It was owned by Simon Witkowski who figured in the turbulent Reconstruction Era. Private.

On U. S. 65, just south of Milliken.

Van Fossen House

This one-story frame cottage is set on huge cypress blocks. Among the original furnishings is a rosewood suite which is supposed to have been made for the Napoleon House in New Orleans, when Mayor Girod offered his home as a refuge for the deposed emperor. Private.

Off U. S. 65, on the River Road, eight miles south of Milliken.

Arlington

This two-story house has the first story of brick, and the second of cypress — both of which have wide verandas extending across the front and around the east end of the house. ARLINGTON is majestically situated in a grove of ancient magnolia, live oak, cypress, cedar and black walnut trees.

Built about 1841 for Mrs. T. R. Patten, the house was originally a one-story building of cypress. A later owner, Gen. Edward Sparrow, senior senator from Louisiana in the Congress of the Confederacy, raised it and added an understory of brick.

During the Civil War, it was used as headquarters for many Union officers, including Macpherson, McMillan and MacArthur. According to tradition, the house was also used by General Grant when he visited Lake Providence. ARLINGTON stands near Grant's Canal — the forlorn monument to the unsuccessful attempt by that general to build a canal across DeSoto Point, to enable his gunboats to avoid the Confederate shore batteries during the siege of Vicksburg in 1863. Private.

Off U. S. 65, east of Lake Providence, across Grant's Canal.

Crescent Plantation House

Gabled roof and eight square columns supporting a wide gallery are features of this famed house. The great front doorway, flanked by French windows that extend almost to the top of the 14-foot ceiling, enters upon a spacious hall. Original brass knobs and locks of the door are in use, as are its transoms of stained glass which were all imported from Europe.

Inside, a spiral stairway with a mahogany railing ascends from the rear of the hall to the second floor. The plastered walls and ceiling ornaments are well-preserved.

The original house was constructed about 1832, and the present front section was added in 1855. Private.

On U. S. 80, four-and-one-half miles east of Tallulah.

TOUR 11A

Carpenter House

A one-story frame structure set on brick pillars with six square wooden columns and a shingled, gabled roof, CARPENTER HOUSE was a popular inn on the Vicksburg-Monroe stagecoach line during the 1850's.

According to legend, the house was named for Samuel Carpenter — leader of the Kentucky-Cave-in-Rock Bandits, who was slain near Vidalia, La., in 1803. Private.

Located on U. S. 80 — La. 17, at Delhi, 20 miles west of Tallulah.

D'Anemour-O'Kelly House

Reputed to be the oldest house in Monroe, the one-and-one-half-story frame structure was built about 1790 by M. D'Anemour on land granted to de la Baume.

The newer portions of the home were added in 1870 when Col. Henry O'Kelly purchased and renamed it.

The home has wide galleries, square white columns and green shutters. It is of hand-hewn cypress construction in which no nails were used, and its massive cypress doors

116

afforded its early inhabitants protection from attacking hordes.

It is presently owned by Mr. and Mrs. Charles M. Mitchell and Miss Mary O'Kelly. Private.

It has been remodeled and moved to Horseshoe Lake Road, off U. S. 165, about 12 miles north of Monroe.

Little Red Brick House-Fort Miro

Although not a plantation home, this structure occupies a site near the historic Fort Miro, the original Spanish fort in this area. Built in 1790, Fort Miro was a stockade fortification 190 feet by 140 feet and served as protection against the Indians. After the city was renamed Monroe, Fort Miro played a lesser role and the land passed through the hands of several individuals.

The present structure was built in 1840 by Samuel Kirby. Previous owners of the land were Dr. C. H. Dabbs, Hyppolite Pargoud and Don Juan Filhiol.

Preserved by the Monroe Committee of the National Society of Colonial Dames, the building houses valuable documents and relics from Monroe's history. On display are an original deed box which held land grants, a crystal decanter once owned by Governor Roman, a piece of silk from a dress worn by Martha Washington, a souvenir towel from Washington's inauguration and other local relics.

Private.

At 520 South Grand Street.

Wooten House

The house is simple in design, one-story in height, with six square wooden columns across the long front gallery.

Immense handmade iron hooks hang from the ceiling, from which jugs filled with water were suspended and swung back and forth by little Negro slaves to cool the drinking water.

WOOTEN HOUSE was once the overseer's home for Lower Pargoud Plantation.

It is located at 2111 South Grand Street, in Monroe.

Upper Pargoud

A frame structure of two stories with gabled roof, broken by wide three-windowed dormers and supported by classic columns, it is considered one of the oldest plantation houses in Ouachita Parish.

It was built in the early 19th century as an overseer's home by Hypolite Pargoud, one of Monroe's first wealthy planters and merchants. About 400 yards north of the plantation house, between the levee and Ouachita River, is the Pargoud Indian Mound. According to tradition, the mound is the burial place of Wichita, beautiful daughter of the Indian chief, Ucita. She died after she had been deserted by Juan Ortego, a member of de Navarez's expedition who had married her in gratitude for saving his life. Private.

At the end of Island Drive, in Monroe.

Layton Castle

This huge structure is not antebellum, but is listed here because of its historical interest. Incorporated within its dull-pink brick walls is part of the Old Bry House — built about 1810 by Judge Henry Bry, a prominent early settler of Monroe. The principal architectural feature of this house is a tower worthy of feudal Europe.

LAYTON CASTLE was built in 1910 by the widow of Robert Layton II (grandson of Henry Bry). The house contains treasured lithographs and chromolithographs of pictures painted by John James Audubon, and a small folio of his works.

Judge Bry was a close friend of Don Juan (Jean Baptiste) Filhiol, and often entertained Audubon. He led the delegation that welcomed the steamboat "James Monroe" — the first steamboat to sail up the Mississippi — to Fort Miro in 1819, and renamed the settlement, Monroe, in honor of the occasion.

LAYTON CASTLE has the charm of an Old World manor house and a collection of rare camellias which have grown to enormous size in its gardens. About 70 feet from the house, in a grove of trees and shrubs, is the cemetery of the old Bry homestead, enclosed by a brick wall. A dilapidated little brick house, located against the west cemetery wall, housed Judge Bry's silkworms. Some of the mulberry trees he planted are still thriving. Private.

In the 1300 block of South Grand Street, Monroe.

Huey House

This two-story frame house, set upon pillars of native rock, was built before the War Between the States by John Huey. It was also used as an inn on the Monroe-Shreveport stagecoach line. Private.

On U. S. 167, just north of Ruston.

Davis House

Located near Lake D'Arbonne, this raised one-story house was built about 1890 by James Wade, ancestor of the present owners. Construction is of cypress. Private.

Located in the D'Arbonne community on La. Hwy. 33, eight miles south of Farmerville.

Read Home

Probably the oldest home in Farmerville, this residence is now the home of Mr. and Mrs. P. L. Read. Private.

At 801 North Main Street.

Edgewood

One of the most spectacular homes in North Louisiana, this 12-room landmark also is known as the BAUGHMAN PLANTATION HOME. Built in 1902 by Jefferson Baughman, it is situated on a 3,000-acre stand of timber.

The entire front of the rambling structure is galleried. Two staircases, one curved, one straight, provide access. The most distinctive feature, however, is a towering turret at the center. Materials for construction were said to have been transported by wagon from Monroe. Private.

Located a mile west of Farmerville on La. Hwy. 2.

Hopkins Home

This two-story structure with two fireplaces on one side occupies a prominent place in musical history. Ann Porter Harrison, the composer of "In the Gloaming," was employed in 1854 to teach music to the children of the residents, Mr. and Mrs. Elias George. A broken romance, and perhaps the beauty of the home, led her to write "In the Gloaming." Private.

At Marion, in northeast Union Parish.

TOUR 11B

Concord

This two-story house, set on brick pillars, was once occupied by Richard Graham Benjamin — son of the man who built HOMESTEAD. The house has square wooden pillars across its gallery, and was built prior to the War Between the States. Private.

Off U. S. 65, one-half mile beyond HOMESTEAD.

Winter Quarters

(OPEN TO PUBLIC)

This one-and-one-half story, 19-room frame house set on high brick pillars was built on one of the last Spanish land grants to be given in Louisiana. A gallery with five

Winter Quarters

121

large square columns fronts the house. Originally a three-room hunting cottage used as "winter quarters," the home was taken over by Grant's troops during the Civil War.
Open daily, 9-5. Nominal entrance fee.

La. 608, on Lake St. Joseph.

Lakewood

Established in 1854 by Capt. A. C. Watson, commander of Watson's Battery during the War Between the States, LAKEWOOD is constructed in the typical architectural style of the period.

When Watson left his home to join General Lee, he buried some $20,000 on the grounds of LAKEWOOD — most of which he recovered after he returned. A descendant uncovered the missing jar containing $5,000 in 1928. Private.

On the Lake Bruin Road, in the vicinity of Lake Bruin.

Bondurant House

This one-story house was originally the second story of Pleasant View, a plantation built in 1852 and moved back from the river in the 1880's.

The house was shelled during the War Between the States, during which Mrs. Bondurant had more than 100 bales of cotton burned to keep them from falling into the hands of the Union forces.

When the house was moved, cannon balls were found lodged in the timbers. Bullet holes can yet be seen in the front door and the low half-doors that open on French windows. Private.

On Second Street, in St. Joseph.

Davidson

This elegant house was built around an original log dwelling about 1850 by Joseph Moore, an early Louisiana planter, for his daughter, Mrs. Carrie Moore Davidson. Now owned by her daughter, Miss Marjorie Davidson, the home contains many original family furnishings. Private.

At St. Joseph.

TOUR 11C

Whitehall

This is a Creole cottage, built prior to the Civil War. It is now owned by former Governor James A. Noe. Private.

On U. S. 165, south of Monroe.

Filhiol House

This one-story frame house features lumber milled from nearby woods, and hinges and locks wrought in the plantation's own blacksmith shop. It has square cypress pillars on the front porch and a fanlight above the front door.

It was built in 1855 by John B. Filhiol, wealthy planter and grandson of Jean Baptiste (or Don Juan Bautista) Filhiol — commandant of Fort Miro, Postes des Washitas (Ouachita Post) and original founder of Monroe.

The inside woodwork in the front room is carefully joined with wooden pegs; no nails were used. Large rafters, smoothed and painted, eliminated the need for a finished ceiling. The dining room is designed to resemble the dining salon of an old river packet.

When additions were made on the original house, Filhiol imported a French cabinetmaker to give the interior an authentic French look.

Among its possessions is an old culverin — a firearm, bound with iron hoops and mounted on a wooden block — which was taken from the armament of Fort Miro, the previous name for the Monroe site. Private.

Off U. S. 165, 12 miles south of Monroe, near Buckhorn Bend on the Ouachita River.

Synope

This raised Creole cottage has graced the Ouachita River area for more than 150 years. The interior features four fireplaces and 12-foot high ceilings. Situated on a 1,500-acre plantation, it is surrounded by a landscaped five-acre garden. Private.

U.S. 165, 10 miles north of Columbia.

Synope

Breston Plantation Home

The oldest home in Caldwell Parish, this residence may have been constructed as early as the 1790s, although a construction date in the 1830s is more probable. The land on which the one-and-one-half story, dormered residence stands was bought in 1837 by Jean Baptiste Bres, who had come to Louisiana from France in 1799. Private.

On east bank of the Ouachita River, five miles north of Columbia at Riverton.

Waverly

This old residence was built on land settled in 1815 and once was part of a 1,000-acre plantation owned by John Pierre Landerneau, Sr., and Jacques Chale. Private.

In northern Caldwell Parish, on the east bank of the Ouachita River.

INDEX